YOUR POWER
in the
HOLY SPIRIT

*"He that believeth on me,
the works that I do shall he do also;
and greater works than these shall he
do; because I go unto my Father."*
—John 14:12 (KJV)

John G. LAKE
Compiled by Roberts Liardon

WHITAKER
HOUSE

All Scripture quotations are taken from the King James Version of the Holy Bible. All words in **bold italics** within Scripture quotations are the emphasis of John G. Lake.

Publisher's Notes:
The sermons, letters, and pamphlets contained here have been excerpted from *John G. Lake: The Complete Collection of His Life Teachings*, which was compiled by Roberts Liardon, originally published by Albury Publishing, and is currently published by Whitaker House. Both Albury Publishing and Whitaker House have made all possible efforts to secure permission and to insure proper credit was given for every entry within this book. The words, expressions, and sentence structure of the text have been gently edited for clarity and readability.

This book is not intended to provide medical advice or to take the place of medical advice and treatment from your personal physician or other qualified health care professionals. Neither the publisher nor the compiler nor the compiler's ministry takes any responsibility for any possible consequences from any action taken by any person reading or following the information in this book. If readers are taking prescription medications, they should consult with their physicians and not take themselves off prescribed medicines without proper medical supervision. Each reader is solely responsible for the consequences of his or her personal choice concerning consultation with physicians or other qualified health care professionals.

YOUR POWER IN THE HOLY SPIRIT

Compiled by Roberts Liardon
Roberts Liardon Ministries
www.robertsliardon.com

ISBN: 978-1-60374-163-7
Printed in the United States of America
© 2010 by Roberts Liardon

Whitaker House
1030 Hunt Valley Circle
New Kensington, PA 15068
www.whitakerhouse.com

Library of Congress Cataloging-in-Publication Data

Lake, John G.
  Your power in the Holy Spirit / by John G. Lake ; compiled by Roberts Liardon.
    p. cm.
  Summary: "A compilation of John G. Lake's sermons and other published materials on the subject of the Holy Spirit, with special focus on the believer's power to minister when baptized in the Holy Ghost"—Provided by publisher.
  ISBN 978-1-60374-163-7 (trade pbk. : alk. paper) 1. Holy Spirit—Sermons. I. Liardon, Roberts. II. Title.
  BT122.L35 2010
  234'.13—dc22
                                        2010000141

4 5 6 7 8 9 10 11 12 ⨆⨆ 18 17 16 15 14 13

Contents

Chapter One

The Baptism in the Holy Ghost

Booklet

Reprinted from "The Comforter" of September 1910
Published by The Apostolic Faith Mission
Tabernacle's Printing Works
Johannesburg, South Africa

But sanctify the Lord God in your hearts: and be ready always give an answer to every man that asketh you a reason of the hope that is in you with meekness and fear. (1 Peter 3:15)

B ecause...

- The Rev. S. J. Du Toit, minister of the Dutch Reformed Church, challenged the brethren of the Apostolic Faith Mission to meet him and publicly defend, in open debate, the teaching believed and disseminated by them.

- The Rev. S. J. Du Toit is considered one of the ablest and most skillful debaters in Africa.

- It was at the Dutch Church, Somerset East, Cape Colony, during 1910, that the Reverend gentleman, according to a Graaff-Reinet paper,

"Met his Waterloo" at the hands of two Apostolic Faith Brethren from Johannesburg. To God be the praise.

...We give our readers the more important features of that address of Brother Lake on the baptism in the Holy Ghost (the Holy Spirit).

PROGRESSIVE REVELATION OF GOD

This is a subject so profound and so comprehensive that to intelligently understand it, we must view it from the scope of continuous and progressive revelation. Like water baptism of the Christian believer, the operations of the Holy Ghost must be apprehended in its successive stages of revelation; otherwise, we shall be unable to distinguish between the operation of the Spirit in the Old Testament and the baptism of the Holy Ghost in the New Testament.

A successive dispensation of God never destroys a preceding one. On the contrary, it conserves its spirit but broadens its scope.

This is obviously seen by comparing the Patriarchal, Mosaic, and Christian dispensations.

In the Patriarchal dispensation, we see God appearing to man at long intervals. Abraham furnishes the best example. God appeared to him at intervening periods of time, twenty and forty years apart. The Patriarchal age may therefore be designated the dispensation of God's revelation *to* man.

There is a perceptible advance under the Mosaic dispensation to a deeper, clearer, and more pronounced manifestation of God. He was ever present in the pillar of cloud and the pillar of fire. Afterwards, His visible presence abode in the Shekinah glory overshadowing the mercy seat. This was God *with* man, not *to* man, as in the Patriarchal dispensation; but rather, God leading, guiding, directing, forgiving, sanctifying, abiding *with* man.

Coming to the Christian dispensation, we obtain a clearer and more palpable revelation of God than in the preceding Mosaic dispensation.

THE CLIMAX

Revelation teaches its climax in this, the Christian dispensation. God *in* man! For the baptism of the Holy Ghost is the actual incoming of that Third Person of the glorious Trinity to live in man. This, then, brings us to where we can see the purpose of God in revealing Himself to man by progressive stages of revelation.

As the Christian dispensation supersedes and eclipses all other dispensations, so the real Christian is to excel all who have preceded him. He is the culminating point of God's effort for mankind. Man is not only to be forgiven, but also is to be cleansed through the blood of Jesus from the nature of sin, from the evil principle that causes him to transgress. This cleansing from "inbred sin" (termed also the "carnal mind," the "old man," the "man of sin") is the actual and experiential taking out of our breast the desire for sin. All correspondence with sin is severed, and the old self-life is laid in glad and willing surrender on the altar of Christ.

GOD WANTS A CLEAN TEMPLE

This inner heart cleansing that John and the disciples of Jesus demanded before they would baptize a man is the necessary preparation for the baptism of the Holy Ghost. Our holy God must have a holy dwelling place. O wondrous salvation! Wondrous atonement! Wondrous Christ! Man—born in sin and shaped in iniquity (see Psalm 51:5)—forgiven, cleansed, purified by the blood of Jesus, and made a habitation, a dwelling place of God through the Spirit.

The redemption that Jesus Christ wrought out on Calvary restores to man all the privileges and prerogatives forfeited by the fall.

Christ hath redeemed us from the curse of the law, being made a curse for us: for it is written,

Cursed is every one that hangeth on a tree: that the blessing of Abraham might come on the Gentiles through Jesus Christ; that we might receive the promise of the Spirit through faith.

(Galatians 3:13–14)

This reveals to us God's purpose in our salvation. We must be prepared by the blood of Jesus Christ to become the habitation of God, *"In whom ye also are builded together for an habitation of God through the Spirit"* (Ephesians 2:22). Again in 1 Corinthians 6:19, Paul asked in astonishment: *"What? know ye not that your body is the temple of the Holy Ghost which is in you?"*

A MARVELOUS FACT

The personal coming of the Holy Ghost into human consciousness is a marvelous fact of God's manifestation in history! His coming was just as definite and conspicuous as the advent of Christ. Was the Christ's coming proclaimed by angel voices and chanted by *"a multitude of the heavenly host praising God"* (Luke 2:13)? Equally, was the Holy Spirit's advent attested by His *"bodily shape like a dove"* (Luke 3:22), and by the *"sound from heaven as of a rushing mighty wind,"* and by the appearance unto them of *"cloven tongues like as of fire"* (Acts 2:2, 3).

Heavenly dove, tempest roar, and tongues of fire crowning the hundred and twenty were as convincing as the guiding star and midnight shouts of angel hosts.

THE PROMISE GIVEN AND REALIZED

In John 16:7, the promise of the Holy Ghost is explicitly given by Jesus:

Nevertheless I tell you the truth; it is expedient for you that I go away: for if I go not away, the Comforter will not come unto you; but if I depart, I will send him unto you.

"If I depart, I will send him unto you." That promise was realized on the day of Pentecost after the disciples had tarried, according to the command of Jesus, *"with one accord in prayer and supplication"* (Acts 1:14).

THE BELIEVER'S IDENTIFICATION WITH CHRIST IN HIS DEATH AND RESURRECTION

Between the day the Holy Ghost was promised and the event of His coming at Pentecost, there was the great day of our Lord's crucifixion. It behooved Christ to suffer in order to make the gift of the Holy Ghost possible to man. There is also a day of crucifixion to the Christian. He must be crucified with Christ: the "old man" must be nailed to the cross, for in no other way can we be delivered from sin. Dying to sin is a real act, a genuine experience.

"Buried with him by baptism into death" (Romans 6:4) and *"being made conformable unto His death"* (Philippians 3:10), we become partakers of the resurrection life of Jesus. The new life of power and victory in God becomes ours, and we are elevated through Christ into His own resurrection life, in actual spiritual experience.

Just as necessary as the crucifixion or the resurrection is the ascension. Jesus ascended into heaven. He sits at the right hand of the Father. According to the promise, He sends down the Holy Ghost, who is also called the Spirit of Jesus, the Spirit of Christ, and the Holy Spirit in the Bible. The Holy Ghost entering into us, taking possession of our personality, living in us, moving us, controlling us, and lifting us into heavenly experiences in Christ Jesus is the baptism in the Holy Ghost, through which we become participators in the ascended life of Christ in glory.

A PERSONAL RECEPTION OF A PERSONAL HOLY GHOST

The outpouring of the Holy Ghost is not only dispensational, but His reception into the heart is to be the personal, conscious experience of every Christian who has sought the enduement of power from on high. The first Pentecostal experience is given in the second chapter of Acts:

> *There came a sound from heaven as of a rushing mighty wind.... There appeared unto them cloven tongues like as of fire.... They were all filled with the Holy Ghost, and began to speak with other tongues, as the Spirit gave them utterance.* (Acts 2:2–4)

Speaking in tongues is the voice of God. It is God speaking through us.

Note: At this point the Holy Ghost spoke through Brother Lake in an unknown tongue. (See 1 Corinthians 14:2.) The congregation was asked to engage in silent prayer for the interpretation of the words spoken in tongues. (See 1 Corinthians 14:13.) Immediately, God answered. The interpretation was as follows:

Interpretation of a Message in Tongues

Christ is at once the spotless descent of God into man, and the sinless ascent of man into God, and the Holy Ghost is the agent by whom it is accomplished.

Bless God! He is the Christ, the Son of God. His atonement is a real atonement. His blood cleanses from all sin. Man again becomes the dwelling place of God.

WHAT ABOUT MANIFESTATIONS?

Let us now consider some of the wonderful manifestations of God to His people in the New Testament, under the baptism of the Holy Ghost. We will take up the tenth chapter of the Acts of the Apostles.

Cornelius, a Gentile centurion living in Caesarea, has a vision. An angel appears to him. The angel speaks to him a comforting message from God. This heavenly messenger also gives him the address of Peter the apostle, who was down at Joppa preaching Jesus, healing the sick, and restoring dead Dorcas to the widows who lamented her. Cornelius is commanded to send for Peter: *"He shall tell thee what thou oughtest to do"* (Acts 10:6).

Two trusted servants and a devout soldier are immediately dispatched to Joppa for Peter. On the following day, as these messengers drew nigh unto the city, Peter was praying and, in a trance, saw a vision. Through this vision God taught him a very necessary and effective lesson on the brotherhood of man and removed from his heart certain inherent and racial prejudices that Peter, as a Jew, had to the preaching of the gospel to the Gentiles.

Think of it, the great Peter in a trance! If I were to fall on the floor in a trance at the present moment, I have no doubt that nine-tenths of this audience would affirm that it was a case of hypnotism—that my opponent, Brother Du Toit, had hypnotized me.

While Peter thought on the vision, he received a message through the Spirit, saying: *"Behold, three men seek thee. Arise therefore, and get thee down, and go with them, doubting nothing: for I have sent them"* (Acts 10:19–20).

THE SIGN OF TONGUES

Peter accompanied the three men to Caesarea. He preached the gospel to the gathering at the house of Cornelius. The whole company was baptized in the Holy Ghost, *"And they of the circumcision which believed were astonished, as many as came with Peter, because that on the Gentiles also was poured out the gift of the Holy Ghost"* (verse 45). How did they know they were baptized in the Holy Ghost? *"For they heard them speak with tongues, and magnify God"* (verse 46). This glorious Holy Ghost service ended in a water baptism of those who had already been baptized in the Holy Ghost.

PAUL SPEAKS TO US

In the twenty-second chapter of Acts, we read Paul's account of his conversion from Judaism to become a disciple of Jesus Christ. A party of horsemen (Saul and certain officers of the law) is on the way to Damascus. Saul holds a commission to arrest all who call on the name of Jesus. Suddenly, there shone from heaven round about them a light greater than the light of the sun. *"And they that were with me saw indeed the light, and were afraid; but they heard not the voice of him that spake to me"* (Acts 22:9).

In the twenty-sixth chapter of Acts, Paul says further:

> *When we were all fallen to the earth* [think of it—the whole party fallen to the earth], *I heard a voice speaking unto me, and saying in the Hebrew tongue, Saul, Saul, why persecutest thou me?* (Acts 26:14)

Who is the speaker? *"I am Jesus whom thou persecutest"* (Acts 26: 15).

TRANCES, VISIONS, REVELATIONS

In order to understand the full force of this incident, as well as to learn the source of Paul's wonderful ministry and of his profound insight into spiritual things, we must find out where he obtained his knowledge of the gospel. Was it communicated to him by the other apostles who had been with Jesus during His earthly ministry? No. It was revealed to him in trances and in visions. He received the knowledge of it directly from the ascended and glorified Christ Himself.

> *But I certify you, brethren, that the gospel which was preached of me is not after man. For I neither received it of man, neither was I taught it, but by the revelation of Jesus Christ.*
>
> (Galatians 1:11–12)

MORE VISIONS

In Acts 22:12, Paul tells of Ananias coming to see him. How did Ananias know Paul was there? The mystery is explained in Acts 9:

> *And there was a certain disciple at Damascus, named Ananias; and to him said the Lord in a vision, Ananais. And he said, Behold, I am*

here, Lord. And the Lord said unto him, Arise, and go into the street which is called Straight, and enquire in the house of Judas for one called Saul, of Tarsus: for, behold, he prayeth.

(Acts 9:10–11)

And now the Lord tells Ananias what Paul had seen:

And hath seen in a vision a man named Ananias coming in, and putting his hand on him, that he might receive his sight.

(Acts 9:12)

In the next verse, Ananias talks with the Lord. Do you know anything of such revelations, of such communion or talks with God? If not, get the baptism of the Holy Spirit like the early Christians had, and their knowledge and experiences in God shall be yours. Men say to us, "Where do you get your insight into the Word of God?" We answer, "Where Paul and Peter obtained it, that is, from God through the Holy Ghost."

Ananias went as the Lord directed him and found Paul. Ananias laid hands on him, and he received his sight. He was baptized in water and also in the Holy Ghost and spoke in tongues *"more than ye all"* (1 Corinthians 14:18).

Now, look again at Acts 22:14. Ananias is speaking to Paul:

17

And he said, The God of our fathers hath cho-sen thee, that thou shouldest know his will, and see that Just One, and shouldest hear the voice of his mouth. (Acts 22:14)

I want you to notice the phrases "**see** *that Just One*" and "**hear** *the voice of his mouth.*"

TRANCE DEFINED

When did Paul see that Just One? When did he hear the voice of His mouth? The first mention—following Ananias's prophetic words in Acts 22:14—of Paul's seeing and hearing the Just One was when he was in a trance after he had returned to Jerusalem:

And it came to pass, that, when I was come again to Jerusalem [three years after Ananias had prophesied], *even while I prayed in the temple, I was* **in a trance**; *and saw him* [Jesus] *saying unto me, Make haste, and get thee quickly out of Jerusalem: for they will not receive thy testimony concerning me.*

(Acts 22:17–18)

Now, what is a trance? In a trance, the Spirit pre-dominates over the mind and body, and for the time being, the control of the individual is in the Spirit. Our ignorance of spiritual manifestation is such that

18

even ministers of religion have been known to say that such experiences and conditions are of the devil.

Now, let us see when Paul first heard and saw the Just One—when he received his commission to preach—and his condition and attitude at the time. (See Acts 26:12, 16–18.) Paul received his preaching commission while lying on the ground in the dusty roadway near Damascus in a trance, having been ushered into that state by the power and glory of the heavenly light shining around him. Now, if we were to see someone lying on the road talking to an invisible "somebody," no doubt in our ignorance we would send for an ambulance or the police. But this is where Paul received his commission and appointment as preacher and apostle to the Gentiles.

Note: Receiving revelation from the Lord does not require being in a trance state, as Paul clearly said: *"But I certify you, brethren, that the gospel which was preached of me is not after man. For I neither received it of man, neither was I taught it, but by the revelation of Jesus Christ"* (Galatians 1:11–12).

MANIFESTATIONS OF THE SPIRIT

From this we are able to perceive and understand in a measure the operations of God upon those who come under the power of the Holy Ghost. And now, beloved, is the Holy Ghost in the church today? Verily, yes. But you say, "We don't see Him work in this way in our church!" Why? Because you say, "All these things were for apostolic days." Can you find anywhere in the Scriptures that the gifts of the Holy Ghost were withdrawn from the church of Christ? There is no biblical authority for such an assertion, but rather we read, *"The gifts and calling of God are without repentance"* (Romans 11:29).

THE GIFTS

I have preached in four different countries, and, with one exception, no Christian minister has been able to name me the nine gifts of the Holy Spirit. These gifts are enumerated in 1 Corinthians 12:8–11. I was very pleased to hear Brother Du Toit read them at the commencement of this service. It shows that people are beginning to read and to think along these lines. The gifts of the Holy Ghost are:

1. Wisdom

2. Knowledge

3. Faith

4. Gifts of healing

5. Working of miracles

6. Prophecy

7. Discerning of spirits

8. Diverse kinds of tongues (various languages not by natural acquirement but by the Spirit)

9. Interpretation of tongues

I thank God for these precious gifts of the Spirit, and especially for the gifts of healing. May we all learn to know Christ, not alone as our Savior, but as our Sanctifier and Healer, too!

GOD RESTORES HIS PEOPLE

Beloved, we have seen that the Holy Ghost came at Pentecost and that those gifts were there also. However, through lack of faith, many times we do not see them exercised now.

The Apostolic Faith Mission stands for the obtaining of the Holy Ghost through the personal baptism in Him and the enduement of *"power from on high"* (Luke 24:49), as commanded by Christ, and for which the disciples were commanded to "tarry" before they went forth to preach the gospel. For, *"Ye shall receive power, after that the Holy Ghost is come upon you"* (Acts 1:8).

BAPTISM IN THE HOLY GHOST

Speaking in tongues is the external evidence that the Holy Ghost has taken possession of the body of the believer and, therefore, of the tongue. It is the voice of God speaking through the sanctified lips of the believer.

In Acts 2:4, the hundred and twenty disciples spoke in tongues. In Acts 10:44–48, when the Holy Ghost fell on the Gentiles, Peter commanded that they should also be baptized in water.

> *Can any man forbid water, that these should not be baptized, which have received the Holy Ghost as well as we?* (Acts 10:47)

How did they know they were baptized in the Holy Ghost?

> *For they heard them speak with tongues, and magnify God.* (verse 46)

Speaking in tongues was therefore the evidence of the baptism in the Holy Ghost, by which also Peter claimed the right to baptize them in water, because he knew that only those who were saved could receive the baptism in the Holy Spirit. In Acts 19:1–7, Paul found at Ephesus twelve men who had been baptized unto John's baptism. He rebaptized them into Christian baptism and the name of Jesus Christ. When Paul laid hands on them, the Holy Ghost came upon them, and they spoke with tongues and prophesied.

> *Tongues are for a sign, not to them that believe, but to them that believe not.*
>
> (1 Corinthians 14:22)

Chapter Two

The Forerunner of "God's Latter Rain"

Booklet

*A General Letter to the
Christian Public Pentecost in South Africa
August 1908*

Beloved in Jesus everywhere! In order that the Christian public may be aware of what God is doing in our midst, we have decided to issue this newsletter to inform our friends everywhere of the marvelous way in which God is working, not alone in Johannesburg, Pretoria, Krugersdorp, and other centers, but in many places throughout the entire land, where the Holy Ghost is being poured out upon the people.

On May fourteenth, a party of Holy Ghost-baptized missionaries arrived from America in Johannesburg and at once commenced to conduct meetings in this city, the principal place of meeting being the old Presbyterian Church at the corner of Bree and Von Wieligh Streets. Right from the commencement of these services, the power of God has been greatly manifested in the salvation of sinners of all classes, many of whom have been sanctified and baptized with the Holy Ghost and have spoken in various kinds of tongues as on the day of Pentecost. (See 1 Corinthians 12 and Acts 2.) Also, there have been many cases of miraculous healing of all manner of diseases. Preachers and laymen, young men and young women, old men and old women have alike received from God the baptism of the Holy Ghost and are speaking in tongues and praising God with a new joy and power formerly unknown to them. The universal testimony of those receiving the baptism of the Holy Ghost has been, and is, that God has worked with them, and is working with them, in the salvation and sanctification and healing of others in a degree never before known in their lives. The testimony of one Dutch Christian worker illustrates this point. He says:

I have been a preacher of the gospel for years. Up to the time that I commenced to attend these meetings, I had never been able to lay my hand definitely upon anyone that I was really sure had been converted and saved under my ministry, but since I have found Jesus as my Sanctifier, and since I have received the baptism of the Holy Ghost, and since God has commenced to speak through me in tongues, I have entered into such a nearness with God that now my ministry is all changed. At almost every meeting, persons are either saved, sanctified, or baptized with the Holy Ghost.

This work of God that is being made manifest in our midst is only that which is being manifested at the present time throughout the whole world. In every land, this same outpouring of the Spirit of God upon all flesh is occurring. We believe it to be the scriptural "latter rain" as promised by the Lord. (See Joel 2:23–29 and Acts 2:17–21.)

This outpouring of the Spirit of God is manifesting God's preparation of the world for the soon appearing of Jesus Christ in His second coming. (See James 5:7–8.)

Almost universally, the first words of the first message that the Lord gives to the newly baptized soul, either in tongues or their native language, is, "Repent. Jesus is coming. The time is at hand. Get ready!"

This outpouring of the Spirit is not confined to any group or church or sect. In Johannesburg, we see persons of every denomination and of every religious creed alike seeking God for a real and definite work of grace in their souls, receiving from Him the baptism of the Holy Ghost, for *"The same is He which baptizeth with the Holy Ghost"* (John 1:33; see also Acts 10:44–48).

We find that, in the lives of these baptized children of God, the signs of a real gospel ministry follow, as promised by Jesus in Mark 16:14–20.

We are only telling of things that our eyes have witnessed and our ears heard. The most wonderful messages for the Lord, by the Holy Ghost, have been given through many in our midst. It is not uncommon at any public service for the Holy Ghost to use individuals for messages in tongues, the interpretation invariably following, as occurred in the early church of the first century. (See 1 Corinthians 14.)

It is the intent and purpose of this committee, which is composed of only earnest Christian workers and is entirely nondenominational in its character, to publish a paper (both in Dutch and English) so that the people of South Africa and the world may have the opportunity of knowing for themselves these wonderful workings of God in these latter days; that they, as well as we, may join in prayer to God that a mighty outpouring of His Spirit upon this land may come and that the tide of sin and iniquity which has so swept and cursed this land shall be turned back and a reign of righteousness be manifestly established and that all people and all nations shall get down low at the feet of Christ our King, that God may bless and prepare each and all for the appearing of our Lord. (See John 14:1–3.)

The operations of the Spirit of God are easily identified. (See John 14:12–17, 26 and John 16:7–14.)

These Apostolic Faith missionaries who are now in our midst—Brother and Sister Thomas Hezmalhalch, Brother and Sister John G. Lake, Brother Jacob O. Lehman, and Sister Ida P. Sackett—are humble men and women who unquestionably have been sent of

God to South Africa at this time with this message. They represent no organization, and their ministry is to the people. There is no board behind them. As in all Holy Ghost work throughout the earth, they trust God and God alone for their support. No charges of any kind are made for religious services, prayers for the sick, or otherwise. No salaries are received, each individual relying solely on God for his or her maintenance, as the apostles did in the early days. (See Luke 9:1–6.)

Marvelous testimonies of miraculous healing are invariably heard at the meetings. These meetings are simply evangelical services where the Spirit of God controls—God in many cases using boys and girls as well as older persons to deliver messages and pray with the sick.

Amongst those who have been baptized with the Holy Ghost are Dutch and English, Jews and Gentiles, black and white, and at a recent meeting a Chinese missionary from Canton, who is ministering amongst the Chinese here, received the baptism of the Holy Ghost and spoke in tongues. That the coming of our Savior Jesus Christ is at hand we who have watched the progress of this work verily believe. In all these messages spoken by the Holy Ghost, no times or dates are given, but in every message comes the universal warning: *"Therefore be ye also ready: for in such an hour as ye think not the Son of man cometh"* (Matthew 24:44).

Our purpose in writing this letter is that the people may know what God is doing. We contract no debts of any character, but obey the command of the Lord: *"Owe no man any thing"* (Romans 13:8). Consequently, when funds are needed, we ask God in prayer to send such funds as are necessary. And we ask every Christian man and woman to join us in prayer to the end that God will provide the means with which to publish a paper in both Dutch and English, which will be known as "God's Latter Rain," in order that the testimonies of those who have been saved, sanctified, and baptized with the Holy Ghost—and others who have been miraculously healed by the Lord, and so forth—may be published, that all may know and become partakers in these latter-day blessings.

This is God's evangelization movement. It is not controlled by man or the government of man, and it is no organization of man's promoting. It is the Spirit of God being poured out upon the people. Instances are known where the Spirit of God has fallen upon families in South Africa, where no preacher or teacher has been—God alone, in answer to prayer, baptizing these children of God with the Holy Ghost, filling and thrilling their souls with the joys and powers of the world to come. (See Hebrews 6:1–6.)

The hymn printed below was given to Brother Thomas Hezmalhalch by the inspiration of the Holy Spirit.

Jesus Is Coming
Words by T. Hezmalhalch
Music by F. A. Graves
© 1907 by Thos. Hezmalhalch

Verse 1:
Jesus is coming! Yes, coming for me!
Jesus is coming! His glory I'll see.
The clouds are His chariots; the angels His guard.
Jesus is coming! How plain are His words.

Chorus:
Coming again, coming again,
Jesus is coming, is coming to reign.
The clouds are His chariots,
The angels His guard.
Jesus is coming,
How precious His Word.

Verse 2:
Jesus is coming! O glory divine!
Jesus is coming! The Lord who is mine;
Yes, coming in triumph with shout and with song;
Jesus is coming! The time is not long.

Verse 3:
Jesus is coming! He's not far away!
Jesus is coming! We'll care not to stay;
The clouds as our chariots; the angels our guard;
Jesus is coming! This truth is His Word.

Verse 4:

Jesus is coming! The just shall arise!
Jesus, whose coming we'll greet in the skies;
The world will not see us. With Jesus we've gone,
Singing forever the glad chorus song.

Verse 5:

Jesus is coming! Yes, all then shall know!
Jesus, whose coming has conquered our foe;
In victory we'll meet Him; in triumph we'll rise!
Jesus has come! We will shout in the skies.

Verse 6:

Jesus is coming! O saints, do rejoice!
Jesus is coming! So lift up your voice;
The clouds are His chariots; the angels His guard.
Sing of His coming and tell of His Word.

Verse 7:

Jesus is coming! Let anthems arise!
Jesus is coming! Our God's loving prize;
The world's great Redeemer, the Savior of men,
Jesus has conquered! He's coming to reign.

Chapter Three

My Baptism in the Holy Spirit and How the Lord Sent Me to South Africa

Booklet

Divine Healing Institute • Portland, Oregon

The Call of God

Out of the darkness of night I have called thee,
Into the glorious light of the day,
Into the knowledge of God's own salvation,
Entered through Jesus the Truth, Light, and Way.

He who hath planted within thine own bosom
Conscious salvation through Jesus the Lord,
Now waits to see the result of the ransom
Fulfilled in thee through the Spirit and Word.

Yield then, thy being, like Him, thine own Master,
His way for thee is the way of the cross,
Perfected He, e'en through sorrow and suffering,
Obedient even, even to death.

Here as with Him is the secret of victory,
That, having died, from the grave He arose,

In the new life of power divine and majesty
Triumphing over death, hell, and all foes.

Ascending upward above all the heavens,
Into the realms of glory divine,
Reigning as conquerors sending His Spirit,
Abiding ever in your heart and mine.

Thus in our nature the Spirit of conquest
Presses us forward in God's holy war,
Advancing, compelling, delivering, destroying
All power of darkness wherever they are.

Through death to the victory, through trial to
    conquest,
Through suffering to glory, dominion and power,
Thus Calvary ever becomes the door opened
To Jesus, to heaven, to discipleship now.

MY BAPTISM IN THE HOLY SPIRIT

Eight years had passed after God revealed Jesus the Healer to me. I had been practicing the ministry of healing. During those eight years, every answer to prayer, every miraculous touch of God, every response of my own soul to the Spirit had created within me a more intense longing for an intimacy with and a consciousness of God, like I felt the disciples of Jesus and the primitive church had possessed.

33

Shortly after my entrance into the ministry of healing, while attending a service where the necessity for the baptism of the Spirit was being presented, as I knelt in prayer and reconsecration to God, an anointing of the Spirit came upon me. Waves of holy glory passed through my being, and I was lifted into a new consciousness of God's presence and power.

I ministered for a number of years in the power of this anointing. Answers to prayers were frequent and miracles of healing occurred from time to time. I felt myself on the borderland of a great spiritual realm and consciousness but was unable to enter in fully, so that my nature was not gratified and satisfied with the attainment. Friends said, "You have the baptism of the Spirit; if you did not have it, you could not enjoy such a fruitful ministry as you do," and other statements of this nature. Yet the longing in my soul was to me the evidence that there was a better experience than my soul knew.

Finally, I was led to set aside certain hours of the day that I dedicated to God as times of meditation and prayer. Thus a number of months passed, until one morning, as I knelt praying, the Spirit of the Lord spoke within my spirit and said, "Be patient until the autumn." My heart rejoiced in this encouragement. I continued my practice of meditation and prayer. It became easy to detach my soul from the course of life, so that while my hands and mind were engaged in the common affairs of every day, my spirit maintained its attitude of communion with God. Thus, silent prayer became habitual practice. Indeed, it had been to a great extent all my life.

In the autumn, I was brought into contact with a minister of the gospel who was preaching a clear message of God and the baptism of the Holy Spirit. In my study of the man and his teaching, I was struck with the fact that his interpretation of the Word of God was exceedingly true to what my soul understood as the real spirit of the Word.

Through his teaching, I was led into a deeper and clearer consciousness of God's power to keep the heart of man free from the consciousness of sin. Instead of the usual struggle against evil in my inner life, such a consciousness of God's cleansing power in my inner nature became evident that a joyous, victorious note came into my soul.

At this time, in addition to my work as a minister of the gospel, I was engaged as manager of agents for a life insurance company. During the period of which I now speak, I preached practically every night. After our services, I was in the habit of joining a circle of friends who, like myself, were determined to pray through into God to where we could receive the baptism of the Holy Spirit, as we believed the early disciples had received it.

It was my belief that not only should my spirit ascend into a new consciousness of God's presence, but that the evident and conscious power of God should come upon my life. In my consecration to God, again and again I said, "God, if You will baptize me in the Holy Spirit and give me the power of God, nothing shall be permitted to stand between me and a hundredfold obedience."

I continued to meet with these friends almost every night for months. A blessed woman of God who was visiting in our city and was being entertained at my home, observing the anguish of my spirit, said to me one day, "Come aside and let us pray." As we knelt she said, "As we pray, if God reveals any cause of hindrance to you why you do not receive the baptism of the Spirit, you will tell me, and if He reveals any cause to me, I will tell you." We prayed, and no hindrance was revealed to either of us. Then she said, "We will obey the Word of God and the practice of the early church." Laying her hands on my head, she beseeched God that I might receive the baptism of the Holy Spirit.

A deep calm settled upon me. In the afternoon, a brother minister called and invited me to accompany him to visit a lady who was sick. Arriving at the home, we found a lady in a wheelchair. All her joints were set with inflammatory rheumatism. She had been in this condition for ten years.

While my friend was conversing with her, preparing her to be prayed with, in order that she might be healed, I sat in a deep chair on the opposite side of the large room. My soul was crying out to God in a yearning too deep for words, when suddenly it seemed to me that I had passed under a shower of warm tropical rain, which was not falling upon me but falling through me. My spirit and soul and body, under this influence, were soothed into such a deep, still calm as I had never known. My brain, which had always been so active, became perfectly still. An awe of the presence of God settled over me. I knew it was God.

Some moments passed; I do not know how many. The Spirit said, "I have heard your prayers, I have seen your tears. You are now to be baptized in the Holy Spirit." The seeming rain ceased, but it had left such a calm, such a quiet of God upon me as my words cannot tell. Then currents of power began to rush through my being from the crown of my head to the soles of my feet. These shocks of power increased in rapidity and voltage. As these currents of power would pass through me, they seemed to come upon my head, rush through my body and through my feet into the floor. This power was so great that my body began to vibrate intensely, so that I believe if I had not been sitting in such a deep, low chair, I might have fallen upon the floor.

An overwhelming consciousness of God's presence possessed me. A new rush of power, taking hold of my very flesh, seemed to come from my feet and move upward. My throat and tongue began to move in a strange manner, and I found that I was unable to speak English. Presently, I began to speak in another language, one that I had never learned, by the power of the Spirit.

For years I had been a profound student of psychic phenomena and had observed among different bodies of Christian people various manifestations. Sometimes they would be of the Spirit of God, but other times they were purely psychic. I prayed, "Father, You know that I have witnessed many phases of psychic phenomena. Is this the power of God that is coursing through my being, or is it some characteristic of psychic manifestation? Is it real power, or do I just think it is power? Father, I want to know."

God answered that heart cry in the following manner. At that instant, I observed my friend was motioning me to come and join him in prayer for the woman who was sick. In his absorption, he had not observed that anything had taken place in me. I arose to go to him but found my body was trembling so violently that I had great difficulty in walking across the room, and especially in controlling the trembling of my hands and arms. I was familiar with sick people, having ministered to them for so many years. I knew it would not be wise to thus lay my hands upon the sick woman, as I was likely to jar her.

It occurred to me that all that was necessary was to touch the tips of my fingers on the top of the patient's head, and then the vibrations would not jar her. This I did. At once, the currents of holy power passed through my being, and I knew that it likewise passed through the one who was sick. She did not speak but apparently was amazed at the effect in her body. My friend, who had been talking to her, had been kneeling as he talked to her in his great earnestness. He arose, saying, "Let us pray that the Lord will now heal you."

As he did so, he took her by the hand. At the instant their hands touched, a flash of dynamic power went through my person and through the sick woman, and as my friend held her hand, the shock of power passed through her hand into him. The rush of power into his person was so great that it caused him to fall on the floor. He looked up at me with joy and surprise and, springing to his feet, said, "Praise the Lord, John, Jesus has baptized you in the Holy Ghost!"

Then he took the crippled hand that had been set for so many years. The clenched hands opened, and the joints began to work—first the fingers, then the hand and wrist, then the elbow, shoulder, etc.

These were the outward manifestations, but, oh, who could describe the thrills of joy inexpressible that were passing through my spirit? Who could comprehend the peace and presence of God that filled my soul? The sanctifying power of the Spirit in my very flesh, subduing all my nature unto what I understood was the nature of Christ. The revelation of His will, the unspeakable tenderness that possessed me, a love for mankind such as I never had known—all were born within.

Even at this late date, ten years afterward, the awe of that hour rests upon my soul. My experience has truly been, as Jesus said: "He shall be within you '*a well of water springing up into everlasting life*'" (John 4:14). That never-ceasing fountain has flowed day and night through my spirit, soul, and body, bringing salvation and healing and the baptism of the Spirit in the power of God to multitudes.

HOW THE LORD SENT ME TO SOUTH AFRICA

Shortly after my baptism in the Holy Spirit, a working of the Spirit commenced in me, which seemed to have for its purpose the revelation of the nature of Jesus Christ to me and in me. Through this tutelage and remolding by the Spirit, a great tenderness for mankind was awakened in my soul. I saw mankind through new eyes. They seemed to me as wandering sheep, having strayed far, in the midst of confusion, groping and wandering hither and thither. They had no definite aim and did not seem to understand what the difficulty was or how to return to God.

The desire to proclaim the message of Christ and to demonstrate His power to save and bless grew in my soul until my life was swayed by this overwhelming passion.

However, my heart was divided. I could not follow successfully the ordinary pursuits of life and business. When a man came into my office, though I knew that twenty or thirty minutes of concentration on the business at hand would possibly net me thousands of dollars, I could not discuss business with him. By a new power of discernment, I could see his soul and understand his inner life and motives. I recognized him as one of the wandering sheep and longed with an overwhelming desire to help him get to God for salvation and find himself.

This division in my soul between business interests and the desire to help men to God became so intense that, in many instances, what should have been a successful business interview and the closing of a great business transaction ended in a prayer meeting by my inviting the individual to kneel with me while I poured out my heart to God on his behalf.

I determined to discuss the matter with the president of my company. I frankly told him the condition of soul I found myself in, and its cause. He kindly replied, "You have worked hard, Lake. You need a change. Take a vacation for three months, and if you want to preach, preach. But at the end of three months, $50,000 a year will look like a lot of money to you, and you will have little desire to sacrifice it for dreams of religious possibilities."

I thanked him, accepted an invitation to join a brother in evangelistic work, and left the office, never to return.

During the three months, I preached every day to large congregations and saw a multitude of people saved from their sins and healed of their diseases and hundreds of them baptized in the Holy Ghost. At the end of the three months, I said to God, "I am through forever with everything in life but the proclamation and demonstration of the gospel of Jesus Christ."

I disposed of my estate and distributed my funds in a manner I believed to be in the best interest of the kingdom of God, and I made myself wholly dependent upon God for the support of myself and family and abandoned myself to the preaching of Jesus.

While I was ministering in a city in northern Illinois, the chore boy at the hotel where we were stopping was inquiring for someone to assist him in sawing down a large tree. I volunteered to assist him. While I was in the act of sawing the tree down, the Spirit of the Lord spoke within my spirit, clearly and distinctly: "Go to Indianapolis. Prepare for a winter campaign. Get a large hall. In the spring you will go to Africa."

I returned to the hotel and told my wife of the incident. She said, "I knew several days ago that your work here was done, for as I prayed, the Spirit said to me, 'Your husband is going on.'"

I went to Indianapolis. The Lord directed me in such a marvelous way that, in a few days, I had secured a large hall and was conducting services, as He had directed. About this time, the following incident took place, which has had so much to do with the success of my ministry ever since.

One morning when I came down to breakfast, I found my appetite had disappeared. I could not eat. I went about my work as usual. At dinnertime, I had no desire to eat, and no more in the evening. The next day was similar, and the third day likewise. But toward the evening of the third day, an overwhelming desire to pray took possession of me. I only wanted to be alone to pray.

For days following, this condition remained upon me. I could neither eat nor sleep. I could only pray. Prayer flowed from my soul like a stream. I could not cease praying. As I rode on the street car, I prayed. As soon as it was possible to get a place of seclusion, I would kneel to pour out my heart to God for hours. Whatever I was doing, that stream of prayer continued flowing from my soul.

On the night of the sixth day of this fast that the Lord had laid on me, while I was washing my hands, the Spirit said to me once again, "Go and pray." I turned around and knelt by my bedside. As I knelt praying, the Spirit asked, "How long have you been praying for the power to cast out demons?"

And I replied, "Lord, a long time."

And the Spirit said, "From henceforth, thou shalt cast out demons." I arose and praised God.

The following night at the close of the service, a gentleman came to me and pointed to a large, red-letter motto on the wall, which read, *"In my name shall they cast out devils"* (Mark 16:17). He said, "Do you believe that?"

I replied, "I do."

He said, "Do not answer hastily, for I have gone all around the land seeking for a minister who would tell me that he believed that. Many have said they did, but when I questioned them, I found they wanted to qualify the statement."

I said, "Brother, so far as I know my soul, I believe it with all my heart."

Then he said, "I will tell you why I asked. Two and a half years ago, my brother, who was manager of a large grain elevator, was attending a religious service. He was seeking the grace of sanctification and suddenly became violently insane. He was committed to the asylum and is there today. Somehow, in the openness of his nature, he apparently became possessed by an evil spirit. Physicians who have examined him declare that every function of his body and brain are apparently normal, and they cannot account for his insanity. If you say that you believe in the casting out of demons by the power of God, I will bring him here on Sunday from the asylum, and I will expect you to cast the devil out."

44

I replied, "Brother, bring him on."

Then we knelt and prayed that the officers of the institution would be inclined by the Spirit of God to permit the man to be brought.

On Sunday in the midst of the service, the man came. He was in the charge of his brother, along with an attendant from the institution. His elderly mother was also one of the group. They came in during the preaching service. I stopped preaching and said to the attendant, "Bring him here; let him kneel at the altar." Then I looked over the audience and selected half a dozen persons whom I knew to be people of faith in God. I invited them to come and kneel in a semicircle about the man and to join me in prayer for his deliverance.

When they had knelt and were praying, I stepped from the platform, laid my hands on his head, and in the name of Jesus Christ, the Son of God, commanded the devil that possessed him to come out of him. The Spirit of God went through my being like a flash of lightning. I knew in my soul that that evil spirit was cast out and was not surprised when, in a moment, the man raised his head and spoke intelligently to me. In a few minutes, he arose from the altar and took a seat in the front row beside his mother and brother. He listened to my address in perfect quiet. When the congregation arose to sing, he acted embarrassed because no one had offered him a hymn book. So I stepped down and handed him mine, and he sang the hymn with the rest of the congregation. After the service was dismissed, he remained and talked with me in a perfectly normal manner.

He returned to the asylum. The brother and attendant told of what had taken place. The physicians examined him and advised that he remain for some days until they were satisfied as to whether he was healed or not. On Wednesday, he was discharged. On Thursday, he returned to his home and took up his former position as manager at the grain elevator, a healed man.

Thus, God verified His word to me, and from that day to this, the power of God has remained upon my soul, and I have seen hundreds of insane people delivered and healed.

One day during the following February, my preaching partner said to me, "John, how much will it cost to take our party to Johannesburg, South Africa?"

I replied, "Two thousand dollars."

He said, "If we are going to Africa in the spring, it is time you and I were praying for the money."

I said, "I have been praying for the money ever since New Year's. I have not heard from the Lord or from anyone else concerning it."

He said, "Never mind. Let's pray again."

We went to his room and knelt in prayer. He led in audible prayer, while I joined my soul in faith and prayer with him. Presently, he slapped me on the back, saying, "Don't pray anymore, John. Jesus told me just now that He would send us that two thousand dollars, and it would be here in four days."

A few days later, he returned from the post office and threw out upon the table four five-hundred-dollar drafts, saying, "John, there is the answer. Jesus has sent it. We are going to Africa."

We purchased tickets from Indianapolis, Indiana, to Johannesburg, South Africa, for the entire party. The gift of money had been sent to Brother H. He read me a clause of the letter. As nearly as I can remember, it said, "While I was standing in the bank at Monrovia, California, the Lord said to me, 'Send Brother H. two thousand dollars.' Enclosed find the drafts. The money is yours for whatever purpose the Lord has directed you to use it." I never knew who the writer of the letter was, as he desired no one else to know.

We left Indianapolis on the first day of April, 1898, my wife and seven children and I and four others. We had our tickets to Africa, but I had no money except $1.50 for personal expenses en route. As the train pulled out of the station, a young man ran alongside of the train and threw a two-dollar bill through the window, making

$3.50.[1] A young lady, who had been one of our workers, accompanied us as far as Detroit, Michigan. She needed $10 to purchase her ticket to her destination. As we rode along, I said to my wife, "When we reach Detroit, I will need $10 for Miss W's railway ticket, and I have no money." So we bowed our heads and prayed.

I had never taken any of my family or friends into my confidence concerning my affairs. They were not aware of whether I had money or not. However, when we reached Detroit, several friends were waiting to say good-bye. As I stepped off at the station, my brother took me by the arm and walked across the station with me. He said to me, "I trust you will not feel offended, but all day long I have felt that I would like to give you this," and he slipped a $10 bill in my vest pocket. I thanked him, turned about, purchased the young lady's ticket, and rejoined the party.

Out of my $3.50, we purchased some canned beans and other edibles, which we used on the train enroute to St. Johns, New Brunswick, where we took a ship for Liverpool. On leaving the ship, I gave half of this to our waiter as a tip. We remained a week in Liverpool at the expense of the transportation company, waiting for the second ship.

One day, Mrs. Lake said to me, "What about the laundry for our party?"

---

[1] In today's economy, the equivalent value is approximately $93.

I replied, "Send it to the laundry. I have no money, but perhaps the Lord will meet us before we need to get it." Being very busy, I forgot about it entirely. On the last night of our stay in Liverpool, just after I had retired about midnight, my wife said, "How about the laundry?"

I replied, "I am sorry, but I forgot it."

She said, "Just like a man. But now, I will tell you about it: I knew you did not have any money, and neither did I. I prayed about it, and after praying, I felt that I should go down to the laundry and inquire what the amount of the bill was. I found it was $1.65. As I was returning to the hotel, I passed a gentleman on the street, and presently he said to me. 'Pardon me, but I feel I should give you this,' and he handed me a number of coins. I returned to the laundry, counted it out to the laundryman, and found it was just the amount of the bill."

We rejoiced in this little evidence of God's presence with us. That next morning, we left by train for London and boarded our ship for South Africa that evening.

When I got on the ship, I had an English shilling. I purchased a shilling's worth of fruit for the children when our ship stopped at one of the Canary Islands, and the last penny was gone.

Through my knowledge of the immigration laws of South Africa, I knew that before we would be permitted to land, I must show the immigration inspector that I was the possessor of at least $125. We prayed earnestly over this matter. About the time we reached the equator, a rest came into my soul concerning it; I could pray no more. When I say I felt that we were "prayed up" on that question, Christians who get answers from God will know what I mean.

About eight or ten days later, we arrived in Cape Town Harbor, and our ship anchored. The immigration inspector came on board, and the passengers lined up at the purser's office to present their money and receive their tickets to land. My wife said, "What are you going to do?"

I said, "I am going to line up with the rest. We have obeyed God thus far. It is now up to the Lord. If they send us back, we cannot help it."

As I stood in the line awaiting my turn, a fellow passenger touched me on the shoulder and indicated to me to step out of the line and come over to the ship's rail to speak with him. He asked some questions and then drew from his pocket a traveler's checkbook and handed me two money orders aggregating forty-two pounds sterling, or $200.

I stepped back into the line, presented my orders to the inspector, and received our tickets to land.

Johannesburg is one thousand miles inland from Cape Town. Throughout the voyage and on the train, we earnestly prayed about the subject of a home. We were faith missionaries. We had neither a missions board nor friends behind us to furnish money. We were dependent on God. Many times during the trip to Johannesburg, we bowed our heads and reminded God that when we arrived there, we would need a home. God blessed and wondrously answered our prayer.

Upon our arrival at Johannesburg, Brother H. stepped off the train first. I followed. I observed a little woman bustling up, whom I instantly recognized as an American. She said to Brother H., "You are an American missionary party?"

He replied, "Yes."

She said, "How many are there in your family?"

He replied, "Four."

"No," she said, "you are not the family. Is there any other?"

He said, "Yes, Mr. Lake."

Addressing me, she said, "How many are in your family?"

I answered, "My wife, myself, and seven children only."

"Oh," she said, "you are the family!"

I said, "What is it, madam?"

As I recall, her answer was, "The Lord sent me here to meet you, and I want to give you a home."

I replied, "We are faith missionaries. We are dependent on God. I have no money to pay rent."

She said, "Never mind the rent. The Lord wants you to have a home."

That same afternoon, we were living in a furnished cottage in the suburbs, the property of our beloved benefactor, Mrs. O. L. Goodenough, of Johannesburg, who remains to this day our beloved friend and fellow worker in the Lord. She is now a resident of Florida and has visited us in the West.

Chapter Four

Guidance

Interpretation of Tongues

South Africa, 1908

O, soul, on the highway from earth unto glory,
Surrounded by mysteries, trials, and fears,
Let the life of thy God, in thy life be resplendent,
For Jesus will guide thee, thou need'st never fear.

For if thou wilt trust Me, I'll lead thee and guide thee
Through the quicksands and deserts of life,
    all the way.
No harm shall befall thee; I only will teach thee
To walk in surrender with Me day by day.

For earth is a school to prepare thee for glory,
The lessons here learned you will always obey.
When eternity dawns, it will be only the morning
Of life with Me always, as life is today.

Therefore, be not impatient, as lessons thou art
    learning,
Each day will bring gladness and joy to thee here;
But heaven will reveal to thy soul of the treasure,
Which infinitude offers through ages and years.

For thy God is the God of the earth and heavens;
And thy soul is the soul that He died to save;
And His blood is sufficient, His power eternal;
Therefore rest in thy God, both today and always.

Chapter Five

The Secret of Power

Interpretation of Tongues

Luke 24:49 and Acts 1:8
June 18, 1910
South Africa

He is risen, He is risen! Hear the cry,
Ringing through the land and sea and sky.
'Tis the shout of victory, triumph is proclaimed,
Heralds of God announce it, death's disdained.

Shout the tidings! Shout the tidings! Raise the cry.
Christ's victorious, Christ's victorious cannot die,
For the bars of death He sundered, Satan sees
    that he has blundered,
As the shouts of angels thundered, "He's alive!"

Catch the shout, ye earth-born mortals, let it roll
Till it echoes o'er the mountains from the center
    to the poles,
That the Christ of earth and glory death has
    conquered.
Tell the story, He's the Victor, He's the Victor!
    So am I.

For this reason that my ransom He has paid,
I've accepted His atonement, on Him laid.

He the Lamb of God that suffered all for me,
Bore my sins, my grief, my sickness on the tree.

I am risen, I am risen from the grave,
Of my sins, my griefs, my sickness, and the waves,
Of the resurrection life, and holy power
Thrill my being with His new life every hour.

Now the lightnings of God's Spirit burn my soul,
Flames of His divine compassion o'er me roll.
Lightning power of God's own Spirit strikes
    the power of hell.
God in man, O glory! Glory! All the story tell.

I have proved Him. I have proved Him. It is true.
Christ's dominion yet remaineth; 'tis for you.
Let the fires of holy passion sweep your soul.
Let the Christ who death has conquered take
    control.
He will use you, He will use you. Zion yet has
    saviors still,
Christ the Conqueror only waiteth for the action
    of your will.

Chapter Six

The Vision

Interpretation of Tongues

October 10, 1909

Jesus, Thou King! Glorious and eternal!
Mighty and loving! Powerful and grand!
Who through the blackness and darkness infernal
Guideth and holdeth Thy child by the hand.

Pierced is Thy soul! Grieved is Thy Spirit!
Bleeding Thy feet are. Wounded Thy hand!
Sorrowing Christ, through the veil now uplifted,
See I Thy beckoning with uplifted hand.

Hear I Thy voice as to me Thou now speakest.
See I Thy teardrops silently fall.
Know I the anguish Thy sorrowing spirit
Feels as Thou drinkest this wormwood and gall.

What, Lord, the cause of Thy anguish of spirit?
Why doth this suffering come to Thee now?
Crucified once, on the cross wast Thou lifted?
Have not the cruel thorns pierced Thy brow?

Have not the sins of mankind on Thee rested,
Causing Thy soul in anguish to be torn?

Has not the blood-sweat from Thee been wrested?
Have not Thy saints for the crucified mourned?

Why is it then that again now I see Thee,
Bruised and bleeding, anguished and lone?
Why is the Spirit of Christ now within me,
Witnessing thus of Thy sorrow again?

List, to the answer! Let all the world hear it!
Jesus is speaking! Let all hear His voice!
It is because of the sins of My people;
It is because ye will not heed My voice.

Do ye not bite and devour one another?
Do ye not slay with your tongues and pen
Many of My precious daughters and mothers,
Young men and maidens, e'en boys and old men?

Have ye e'er stood in the fire where they're tested?
Have ye e'er felt of the withering blast?
Know ye how long and how hard they've resisted,
Fighting and struggling unto the last?

Why did ye not stretch your hand out to help them?
Why from the soul did not sympathy flow?
Did not My Spirit within thee say, "Help them
Out of their bondage or darkness or woe?"

Thus am I crucified! Thus My soul anguished!
This is the cause of My sorrow and woe!
This is the reason that Satan has vanquished
Many who once were as pure as the snow!

O, let thy heart in yearning compassion,
Gentleness, meekness, and tenderness mild,
Give of My grace to the soul swept with passion,
Power to live at My feet as a child.

Then shall the gladness and brightness of heaven
Flood thine own spirit and cause thee to move
Among the crushed and the wounded and broken,
Bringing them sunshine, gladness, and love.

Then shall thy spirit in tune with the heavenlies,
Rapturous joys in the Spirit shall know.
Then shall the power of God rest upon thee.
Then in the fruits of the Spirit thou'lt grow.

Then shall the earth know the glory of heaven.
Then shall dominion over death and over hell
Reign in thine own soul, spread as the leaven,
Causing angels and men My praises to swell.

Then shall the Christ o'er the earth be victorious.
Then shall the power of My gospel be known.
My kingdom shall come, eternal and glorious!
United, the heavens and the earth shall be one!

Chapter Seven

Notable Christians in History

Radio Address, Adventures in Religion #1

June 24, 1935

This is the first of a series of addresses on the general subject of "Adventures in Religion." I want to remind you for a few moments of some of the old mystics who were given glimpses into the unseen that it has not been the privilege of the ordinary man to understand.

The first and foremost was St. Francis of Assisi, whom the world has conceded to be one of the most Christlike characters who has ever lived in the world. At a later period came St. John of the Cross, who for ten years seemed to live detached from the world. Today, he has been discovered to be one of the most practical of men.

At a later period, Madam Guyon appeared on the scene, and most every library contains one of her books. The molding of her character was so amazing that it has caused much discussion in the religious world of our day.

We have only, however, to look over the records of our own land to see many others. Such men as Charles

G. Finney, founder of Oberlin College and its first president. He was a practicing lawyer. He was seized with a conviction for sin so pungent that he retired to the woods to pray, and the Spirit of the Lord came upon him so powerfully, so divinely, and took such amazing possession of him that he tells us he was compelled to cry out to God to cease lest he should die. His wonderful ministry in the land is so well-known, his books so frequently found in our libraries, that it is not necessary to discuss him further.

On this list I wish to mention one who is not usually mentioned so lovingly as Finney. John Alexander Dowie was a Scotch boy, educated in the University of Australia. In addition to this, the Lord came to him in his own tabernacle one morning as he sat at his desk. Jesus was accompanied by His mother, the Virgin Mary. He advised Dowie concerning his ministry. Jesus laid His hands upon him, and his ministry was marked by the supernatural from that day on.

It is a matter of public record and one of the most astonishing facts that, on one occasion, he invited all persons who were healed under his ministry to attend a meeting at the auditorium in Chicago. Ten thousand people attended the meeting. At the psychological moment, they all arose and gave testimony to the fact that they were healed. Those who were not able to attend were asked to send in a card, three and a half inches square, telling of their healing. Five bushel baskets were filled with these cards, representing the testimonies of one hundred thousand people. At the psychological moment, these five bushel baskets of cards were spilled over the stage to emphasize the extent and power of God's ministry and blessing to the people.

Again, I want to call your attention to another marvelous life: that of Hudson Taylor, founder of the China Inland Mission. To him the Lord came, not only in personal presence, but also in prophecy concerning the future. It was Hudson Taylor who prophesied the great revival in Wales ten years before it came to pass, giving almost the very day on which it would begin and its power and extent. All this came to pass just as he had outlined it, while he was in the heart of China.

The Welch revival was one of the most remarkable revivals that was ever produced. It was apparently prayed out of heaven by a single little church whose lights were never extinguished for seven years. This indicates that a portion of that congregation was continually in prayer to God, that God would send a revival. And thus it came, the most astonishing and intensely powerful revival. In small churches that would hold perhaps five hundred people, fifty people would be singing the praises of God in one corner, thirty-five people would be down praying, and another group would be praising God and testifying of His power. It was not produced by evangelism, but it was the descent of the Spirit of God on the people. Conviction for sin was so powerful, men knelt in their stores or wherever they were to give themselves to God. Sometimes, while men were drinking in the public houses at the bar, they would cry out to God and give their hearts to Him.

Beginning with that revival, there was a movement of God that spread throughout the world. In our own land, we are particularly and wonderfully blessed by a movement that began New Year's Eve, 1900, which was accompanied by the baptism in the Holy Ghost, and multitudes were baptized in the Holy Ghost.

After that revival, there arose a phenomenal group of men and women. I am going to mention a few. The first I am going to mention is Aimee Semple McPherson. She was a young girl on a farm in Ontario, Canada. She attended a meeting held by a young Irishman, Robert Semple, who was preaching under the anointing of the Holy Ghost. She became convicted of sin, opened her heart to God, found Him, and was baptized in the Holy Ghost. Finally, they were married and went as missionaries to China, where he died of fever. She was left a widow, and soon with a newborn baby. Some friends provided the funds that brought her back to the United States.

Later, she formed an acquaintance with a fine young businessman and decided to settle down and forget all her burning call to the gospel. This she tried to do. Two children were born to them. And then, one day, God came to Aimee in a meeting at Berlin, Ontario, conducted by Reverend Hall. Her early ministry, for a period of about fifteen years, surpassed everything that we have ever seen in any land since the days of the apostles. (A multitude was healed under her ministry.)

Again, I want to call your attention to another unusual man, Raymond Ritchie, who belonged to Zion, Illinois. His father was mayor of Zion City at one time. This boy was tubercular. They did not seem to understand his difficulty. He had no ambition; he could not work like other boys. He was in a state of lassitude. Eventually he found God. We speak of finding God as the old Methodist church spoke of being saved, getting religion, meaning one and the same thing. When a man confesses his sin and God comes into his heart and gives him the peace and consciousness of his salvation, he has found God.

Young Ritchie, after his salvation, was so absorbed in prayer, and the family got sort of worried. The father finally told him he had to get to work and help earn his living. But some woman who understood the boy said, "I have a room you can have." Another said she would provide him with food to keep him alive.

The Great War came on, and the epidemic of the flu followed, when men died by the thousands throughout this United States. He became stirred and began to pray for people, and they were healed. The medical department presently took notice of it, and they sent him to pray for sick soldiers, and they were healed. Very well, he has continued in the ministry from then until now, and he has conducted some of the most wonderful healing meetings that have ever taken place.

Another man God has marvelously blessed and used is Dr. Price. He belongs to our own locality. Price used to live in Spokane. When Dr. Price was baptized in the Spirit, right away he began to manifest a most amazing ministry of healing. I attended one of his meetings at Vancouver, BC. He had four audiences a day and fifteen thousand people in each and people for a block around who could not get inside. All the churches in Vancouver, I think, united with him in that meeting. It was the most amazing meeting I ever saw. The sick people stood in groups of fifty, and he would anoint them with oil, according to the fifth chapter of James, and then pray for them. They were so overpowered by the Spirit, they would fall to the floor, and a great number were healed.

Chapter Eight

A New Wave of Heavenly Experience

Radio Address, Adventures in Religion #2

June 25, 1935

No greater book has ever been given to mankind than the Bible. The amazing things recorded there that men experienced and that men wrought in the name of Jesus Christ, through faith by the power of God, stand forever as an incentive to every man who enters and labors where they did. There is a place in God into which the soul enters, a relationship to God that leaves the registry of heaven here in your heart and that makes it possible for the Spirit of God, through you as His agent, to register in the hearts of others.

Henry Fosdick says, "Until the new theology can produce the sinless character of the old theology, it stands challenged." We believe that. We believe that the old-fashioned salvation through the blood of Jesus Christ and the baptism of the Holy Ghost make possible an experience that no other religious experience in the world has ever been able to produce.

In the year 1900, there came a new wave of heavenly experience to this land and to the world. It began in Topeka, Kansas. It was in a Bible school conducted by Charles Parham. The founding of that school was an amazing thing. He was moved of God to go to Topeka, Kansas. He obeyed the prompting of the Spirit and went to the city. Parham looked all around for a building suitable for a Bible school but found none. One day, a gentleman told him of a residence on the outskirts of the city. It contained twenty-two or more rooms, and it was unoccupied. The owner lived in California. Parham went to see the building, and as he stood looking at it, the Spirit of the Lord said, "I will give you this building for your Bible school."

And he said to himself, "This is the house."

As he stood there, a gentleman came up to him and said, "What about the house?" Parham told him what the Lord had said to him, and the man, being the owner of the house, said, "If you want to use this building for a Bible school for God, it is yours," and he handed him the key without any more ado.

The next day, Parham went to the train station and met a young woman of his acquaintance. She told him that when she was praying, the Spirit of God told her there was going to be a Bible school here and that she should come. She was the first student. Thirty-five students came, all correspondingly directed by the Spirit of God.

This group began a study of the Word of God to discover what really constituted the baptism of the Holy Ghost. After a month of study, they became convinced that there was one peculiarity that accompanied the baptism of the Holy Ghost—speaking in tongues.

They went to seeking the baptism of the Holy Ghost. Parham was not present at the time. On New Year's night at twelve o'clock, 1900, one of the group, a Miss Osmand, a returned missionary, was baptized in the Holy Ghost and began to speak in tongues. In a few days the entire group, with a couple of exceptions, was baptized in the Spirit. When Parham returned and found that the students in his school had been baptized in the Holy Ghost, he himself went down before the Lord, and God baptized him in the Holy Ghost, too.

I want you to keep this story in mind, for it forms the basis of the wonderful experience I want to relate in my next talk.

Chapter Nine

The Wondrous Value of Healing

Radio Address, Adventures in Religion #3

June 26, 1935

For a moment I want to call attention to a challenge that has been distributed widely through the ministry of Henry Fosdick, as I mentioned yesterday. Fosdick has said, "Until the new theology (Pentecostalism) can produce the sinless character of the old theology, it stands challenged."

That is our position. We are reminding you, friends, that God is a miracle God. God is a miracle. Jesus Christ is a miracle. His birth was a miracle. His life was a miracle. His death was a miracle. His resurrection from the grave was a miracle. His ascension was a miracle. His reception at the throne of God by the eternal Father was a great miracle, because God then gave Him the gift of the Holy Ghost and made Him the administrator of the Spirit forever.

Some things can be better taught by relating experiences than in any other way. I might try to impress you with the beauty and wonder of the baptism of the Holy Ghost, but dear friends, I think the relating of a few experiences will make it clearer to your mind than any other way.

I am reminded of an incident that took place on a railway train. Father Neiswender was stricken with a paralytic stroke. He had not been able to sleep for weeks. When they got him on a train to bring him to Spokane, the motion of the train temporarily soothed him, and he fell asleep and dreamed. In his dream, an angel came to him and said, "When you get to Spokane, inquire for a man by the name of Lake. He will pray for you, and God will heal you."

He was directed to our place, and when we prayed for him, he immediately began to use his paralyzed arm and side, but he was not completely delivered. The third time I went to pray, the Lord showed me a blood clot in the spinal cord as large as a bead. I prayed until the blood clot disappeared. No one could explain an incident like that by any natural law. Consequently, we must classify it in the line of miracles *in our day*— not a thousand years ago.

One more incident of this order: A family by the name of Bashor had a lovely boy who became dissatisfied at home and ran away. He went to a farmer where he was not known, gave another name, and worked for him for a year. In the meantime, the family, with the aid of the police, searched everywhere for the boy, but he could not be found. One day, the mother came to me brokenhearted and told me the story. We knelt and prayed and asked God that He would cause that boy to get in touch with his parents. Two days later, she received a letter from the boy. He told her that on the night we had prayed, he went to bed and had an unusual vision. Jesus appeared and talked to him. Jesus said, "I forgive your sins, but I want you to write to your mother and get home to your folks."

The boy was greatly moved, got up, and told the farmer the incident, and the result was that the farmer hitched up his team and brought the boy to his home. The boy is now married and has a nice family and still lives in Spokane. The part of that incident that might interest young folks is this: I was preaching at Mica, Washington, where I related this incident. A young lady in the audience listened to the story, and after the meeting, she said to me, "I would like to get acquainted with that young man." She did, and he is now her husband.

Dear friends, these are some of the things that show us there is a work of God's Spirit that is different from what we are ordinarily accustomed to, and these are the things that make religion real to New Testament Christians. Different ones in the Scriptures were guided by dreams. Joseph was guided by dreams. Some were guided by a voice from heaven. Now we are contending and bringing to your attention that there was an experience provided by the Lord Himself that made that intimacy a possibility—that is, the baptism of the Holy Spirit. I wish I might say that with such emphasis that it would penetrate the deep recesses of your spirit.

One more incident: Over in the woods back of Kellogg, Idaho, lived a family by the name of Hunt. I visited in their home just a little while ago. The aged father was given up to die; the son was very anxious about him. The father kept saying, "Son, I ought not to die." The son had been much in prayer about this matter. One day, the son stood on a logging road, and presently a man appeared a little distance ahead. And as the gentleman approached, he addressed Mr. Hunt, saying, "I am Mr. Lake; I have Healing Rooms in Spokane. If you will bring your father there, the Lord will heal him." He was so impressed that he got his father and brought him to me for prayer. The Lord healed him gloriously, and he lived many more years.

The value of the ministry of healing is not in the mere fact that people are healed. The value of healing is more largely in the fact that it becomes a demonstration of the living, inner, vital power of God, which should dwell in every life and make us new and mighty men in the hands of God.

Chapter Ten

Artillery from Heaven

Radio Address, Adventures in Religion #4

June 27, 1935

When the German army started their famous march on Belgium and France with an army of three million men, they came to the borders only to find that they were met with such a tremendous opposition that for ten full days they were compelled to stay back until they could bring up their heavy artillery. Statesmen of Germany declare that that ten days' delay resulted in their losing the war. France and Belgium were prepared in the meantime to meet the assault.

Jesus Christ, the Son of God, said to His disciples: *"Behold, I send you forth as sheep in the midst of wolves"* (Matthew 10:16), but He did not send them out without being prepared. They were commissioned and empowered by God, for that is what constitutes the baptism of the Holy Ghost. Jesus Christ gave His disciples a big program before He left them. He told them they were not only to preach the gospel to the whole world, but that they were to demonstrate its power.

Go ye into all the world, and preach the gospel to every creature....And these signs shall follow them that believe; in my name shall they cast

73

out devils; they shall speak with new tongues; they shall take up serpents; and if they drink any deadly thing, it shall not hurt them; they shall lay hands on the sick, and they shall recover. (Mark 16:15, 17–18)

These signs shall follow those who *believe*—those who have accepted their work.

Dear friends, men who were going to put a program like that into effect needed heavy artillery from heaven. That is what Jesus undertook to give from heaven. So, He said they were not to go out right away unprepared. Instead, He said:

Tarry ye in the city of Jerusalem, until ye be endued with power from on high. (Luke 24:49)

That enduement from on high is the equipment of every child of God who follows the biblical pattern. We are trying to impress upon the minds of men that one of the greatest adventures in religion that this world ever has found is when men dare to step across the usual boundaries and dare to receive from His hand the baptism of the Holy Ghost, which equips them with the power of God to bring blessings to other lives.

Just for one moment, I want to bring you this fact: The first thing Jesus said would be manifested in the Christian life was, *"In my name shall they cast out devils."* It was the first thing in the Christian experience of the exercise of Christian power that Jesus said would follow the Christian's life. They had power to cast out devils.

Jesus first gave that power to the twelve, then He gave it to the seventy, and then He gave it to the church at large on the day of Pentecost, when the baptism of the Holy Ghost descended upon the hundred and twenty at Jerusalem. Jesus gave them the heavy artillery of heaven—the Holy Spirit baptism.

In our day, within the past thirty years, we have seen such a manifestation of God from heaven as no other century in history ever saw, with the exception of the first four centuries of the Christian era. Beginning with 1900, the Spirit of God began to be poured out in power upon the world so that every country in the world has received this amazing power of God. Men who were ordinary businessmen, men who were scholars and teachers, students, and men from every walk in life found this equipment from heaven by the grace of God, and they stepped out into a great life and ministry for God. This preparation, friends, is not for preachers only, but for the people. Jesus said, *"These signs shall follow them that **believe**."*

Friends, there is an adventure for your soul, the most amazing adventure in all the world. It takes a brave soul to step into the fight of God and receive the equipment He provides. That is no place for a coward.

A cowardly spirit, a spirit that is always hiding, always apologizing for his faith, will never enter there. That is the gate of God. That is the gate into His Spirit. That is the gate into a life of effectiveness for everyone who wants to serve God aright. Friends, you need this equipment to meet the demands of this day.

Sanctification is the cleansing of a man's nature by the indwelling power of the Spirit of Christ, for the purpose of the transformation of the mind and nature of man into the mind and nature of Jesus Christ.

I like John Wesley's definition of sanctification: "Possessing the mind of Christ, and all the mind of Christ."

Chapter Eleven

Miracles Are for Today

Radio Address, Adventures in Religion #5

June 28, 1935

I want to talk to you on the subject of miracles this afternoon. From the year 400 until now, by and large, the church has assumed the attitude that the days of miracles are passed—without any scriptural evidence whatever. They have taught that miracles were to demonstrate the divinity of Jesus and that, therefore, the divinity of Jesus having been demonstrated, there was no longer any need for miracles.

We had a local incident that demonstrates the effect of this teaching. I think my conviction on the matter is that it has done more damage to the Christian faith than any other teaching that has been promulgated. There is a gentleman who works at the Davenport Hotel in Spokane, O. A. Risdon, who is one of the engineers there. He had a son with a deformed head. The top of the head raised up like the ridge of a roof; the forehead and back of the head also were forced out in similar manner, giving the head the appearance of the hull of an upside-down yacht. He was born with what the physicians call a closed head. The boy was always slobbering. The pressure on the brain caused the right side to become paralyzed, and the boy was dumb. He was five years old at this time.

The physicians said there was nothing they could do. Then, in desperation, he appealed to his pastor. The pastor told him that the days of miracles were past, that the Lord did not heal now, and that miracles were given to demonstrate the divinity of Jesus. The father replied, "If Jesus would heal my son, I would be convinced that He is divine now. If He is divine, He could lift this damnation from our house."

Finally, he came to us seeking help. We began to minister to the child. In a few days, we observed that the paralysis began to depart. Instead of walking on one side of his ankles, he began to walk on the foot, and that indicated that the pressure was relieved on the brain. In seven weeks, the child was perfectly well. The bones of the head softened and came down to normal. The paralysis disappeared, and the child began to talk. In three months, he was in the public school. He is a young married man now.

Dear friends, if we had continued to believe that the days of miracles were past, that boy would be in the insane asylum. But we believed that Jesus Christ is the same yesterday, today, and forever, and the boy was healed. It is a delight to believe the *words of Jesus*. I have used this rule in my study of the Scriptures. If there is any question on any Scripture,

I settle it with the words of Jesus. I consider all the Scriptures are a common court of the gospel, but the words of Jesus are the Supreme Court of the gospel. When I want a Supreme Court decision, I appeal to the words of Jesus.

You can read all the words of Jesus in two hours or less in a red-letter New Testament. Make a practice of reading the words of Jesus on any subject that troubles you, and make a compilation of what He says. He ought to be sufficient authority on any question, for the heavenly Father called attention to the fact that He is the Son of God and that we are to hear Him. God declared:

*This is my beloved Son, in whom I am well pleased; **hear ye him**.* (Matthew 17:5)

Chapter Twelve

The Challenger of Darkness

Radio Address, Adventures in Religion #6

July 2, 1935

Jesus Christ came on the scene as the Challenger. We have almost come to believe in our day that He was a sentimentalist and an easy type. However, He was King. He was the Prince of God. He was the Glory of heaven! He was the representative of the eternal Father! He had a mission. He declared the Father. He stepped among the religions of the earth as the Challenger.

Jesus said that there was real sin, that there was real sickness, that there was real death. He was not dodging the issue. He met it foursquare, and He said, "I am bigger than it all. I am the Prince of life." He destroyed sin and obliterated it from the souls of men. He blasted sickness and dissolved it from their system. He raised the dead to life. He challenged the devil, who was the author of death, to destroy Him if he could. He went into the regions of death and conquered and came forth triumphant, so that it became necessary for the Lord to have a new vocabulary. He said after coming forth from the grave,

All power is given unto me in heaven and in earth. Go ye therefore, and teach all nations, baptizing them in the name of the Father, and of the Son, and of the Holy Ghost.

(Matthew 28:18–19)

Sin and sickness and death, the triumvirate of darkness, which Jesus met and overcame, were the original forces of evil in the world, the manifestation of the kingdom of darkness. There never will be a heaven—there never could be one—where these exist. Their destruction is necessary. Jesus realized that, and He came to do what man could not do for himself. That is one of the reasons why men cannot save themselves. All the good works that a man may perform from now to the day of his death will not save him. Sin is of the heart. It is in the nature. Jesus came to reconstruct man's nature and give him, instead of his own evil nature, the nature of God. Sin has made the nature of man vile. Christ came to give him deliverance from this nature and give him a new nature, the divine nature.

Through sin, death entered into this world. (See Romans 5:12.) Death is not a servant of God, not a child of God, nor is it a product of God. Sin is the enemy of God. The New Testament declares, *"The last enemy that shall be destroyed is death"* (1 Corinthians 15:26)—not the last servant or friend, but the last enemy. Death is doomed to destruction by the Lord Jesus Christ. Sin and sickness is incipient death.

That is the reason we do not speak of the things of the Lord and His salvation in moderate tones. We are shouting them to mankind. The spirit of a real child of God challenges darkness, challenges sin, challenges sickness. The Lord Jesus came to destroy sickness and wipe it out of the lives of men to make possible the heaven of God in their hearts and lives now. There can be no heaven where disease and sickness are found. Sin and sickness and death must be blotted out. That is the reason, dear friends, that Christianity is always a challenger. Christianity is a thing of strength. Real religion is a source of power. It is the dynamite of God. The Holy Spirit gives the overcoming grace and strength essential to destroy sin, to destroy sickness, to overcome death.

Chapter Thirteen

Jesus' Program of Deliverance

Radio Address, Adventures in Religion #7

July 3, 1935

I am pleased to greet you today, dear friends, with a real account of one of the marvelous adventures in God. Jesus said, *"Heal the sick, cleanse the lepers, raise the dead, cast out devils: freely ye have received, freely give"* (Matthew 10:8).

Jesus was putting His program of deliverance in force through the church. Christianity is not to be stinted in her giving. She is not to be a beggar. She is to be a giver. She has something from heaven to give that the world does not have. She has something to give that will bring deliverance to the world.

The man is a bold man who undertakes to carry out this program of Jesus. I fear that the Christian who never has faith enough in God to undertake it is of the cowardly type. I am afraid modern Christianity stands indicted at the bar of God for cowardliness because of fear to undertake the program of Jesus.

Friends, this is why we urge upon men the necessity of the baptism of the Holy Ghost. It is the only thing that brings the heavenly equipment to the hearts of men and that makes them equal to this program and the possibility of carrying it out.

I want to talk to you today of a bold soul, and in my judgment, a very extraordinary one indeed. I refer to a gentleman who lives in this city, a preacher of the gospel from the days of his youth, Reverend C. W. Westwood. His home is on Nora Avenue.

A number of years ago, there was born at one of the great hospitals of the city a little child (a girl) from healthy parents, Mr. and Mrs. Young. For many years, Mr. Young had a stall in the Westlake Market. Mrs. Young has been a nurse for many years and also is well-known. When this baby was born, she weighed six and a half pounds. Yet, because of some strange difficulty, the child could not assimilate her food.

When she was nine months old, she weighed only four and a half pounds. The child looked more like a little dried up alligator than like a human being. She finally fell into a state of death and remained in a dying condition. In the meantime, we were called to minister to the child.

Mr. Westwood was assigned to the case. One day, when he went to the hospital as usual to minister to the child, they explained that the child was not there. She had died that morning and was in the dead room [morgue]. He asked if he might see the child, and went into the dead room and took the child down. He sat down on a chair with the baby on his knees. He opened his heart to God and turned the spirit of faith in his heart loose in behalf of the little one. In a little while—and I am saying this with all reverence before God, because I expect to meet this matter when I stand before the great judgment throne—the child revived. Westwood sent for the parents. They took the child from the hospital and put her in the hands of an elderly lady by the name of Mrs. Mason, who nursed her for six weeks. At the end of that period, she was as well as any other child. Her name was Agnes Young.

About a year ago, I received a telephone call from Agnes Young, asking me if I would perform a marriage ceremony for her and her fiancé. This young couple lives in Eugene, Oregon, now.

And so I want to leave with this testimony: God is as good as His Word, and faith in God Almighty brings to pass the very same things today that it always did.

Chapter Fourteen

The Miraculous Realm of the Spirit

Radio Address, Adventures in Religion #8

July 5, 1935

The climax of all adventures was the adventure of Jesus, in delivering men from sin and sickness and death. One cannot measure the Man of Galilee with any tapeline or yardstick that comes from human reasoning. Jesus is outside of the realm of reason. In the first place, His history was written by the prophets ages before He was born. Men can write a better history of Jesus from the Old Testament than they can from the New Testament. In the New Testament, we have simply a little fragment about His incarnation and birth, and then thirty years of silence, except for a little glimpse of Him when He was twelve years of age.

All the books that have been written about Jesus have been written almost entirely about His three years of public ministry, which began with His baptism in the Jordan and closed with His resurrection. Now, men try to write on His preexistence. Here and there one has caught a glimpse of His ministry, seated at the right hand of the Majesty on High.

I want you to see another fact: Every prophecy that was written before His time was in the miracle realm. His incarnation was a real miracle. He was not born under the natural laws of generation. He was conceived of the Holy Ghost. He was a true incarnation—God uniting Himself with humanity. The scenes surrounding His birth—the angelic visitations, the coming of the wise men—all were miracles. The angel's warning to Joseph to flee with the child to Egypt was miraculous. The descent of the Spirit at His baptism was a miracle. From that day until Mount Olivet was a period of miracles. His life among men was a miracle. The new kind of life that He revealed to the world was a miracle.

THE MIRACULOUS MIND OF CHRIST

Jesus' mental processes were miraculous. Our libraries are full of books written by great thinkers like Thomas Edison and others who were incessant thinkers. With Jesus there is something different. He spoke out from the Spirit that dominated His spiritual faculties. The Spirit of Christ ruled His intellect. Gems of divine truth dripped from His lips as honey from the honeycomb. The Sermon on the Mount and great portions in Luke and John are as untouched as when they dropped from the lips of Jesus. Men's writings grow old and out of date. God's truth is ever fresh. Yes, Jesus' words and life and contact with men were miraculous; they are still miraculous.

His death on the cross, His three days in the tomb, His dramatic and startling resurrection, were all miracles. His presence among the disciples on different occasions and, finally, His ascension in the presence of five hundred witnesses were miracles. They do not belong to the reason realm; they belong to the miracle realm. Jesus was in the realm of the Spirit, the realm of faith, the realm where God acts, the realm where the real child of God lives. You see, Christians have been translated out of the realm of human thought and reason into the kingdom of the Son of His love, the realm of the Spirit.

It would be uncharitable if we were to criticize a man of reason who knows nothing about the spiritual realm. Christianity is not the product of human reasoning. Christianity is a divine intervention. Christians are those who have been born from above. They have been re-created. This life of God that comes into their spirit nature dominates the reason so that they have *"the mind of Christ"* (1 Corinthians 2:16) to think God's thoughts and live in God's realm of miracles.

Friends, when a Christian tries to live by reason, he is moving out of God's country into the enemy's land. We belong in the miraculous or supernatural realm.

Christ was a miracle. Every Christian is a miracle. Every answer to prayer is a miracle. Every divine illumination is a miracle. The power of Christianity in the world is a miraculous power. God, help us to realize that ours is a high and holy calling.

Chapter Fifteen

Deeper Purposes of God

Radio Address, Adventures in Religion #9

July 9, 1935

I want to talk to you concerning some of the purposes of God. Among them is God's amazing purpose to baptize men in the Holy Spirit. I think that even among the deepest thinking Christians in our day, little is understood of the real purpose of God in this wonderful experience.

We say to one another that the baptism of the Holy Spirit is God coming into man, that it is God manifesting Himself in man, and other expressions of this type; but it fails to convey to the mind anything like the great purpose of God in His coming into us.

The baptism of the Holy Spirit has among its wonderful purposes the dwelling of God in us, the perfecting of His life in us through His Word in our spirits, through His power in our lives. Speaking in other tongues is the peculiar manifestation of God accompanying the coming of God the Holy Spirit into the life. This was the evidence when the Holy Spirit of God descended on the day of Pentecost at Jerusalem. The Scripture is given in these wonderful words:

*Suddenly there came a sound from heaven as
of a rushing mighty wind, and it filled all the
house where they were sitting. And there appeared unto them cloven tongues like as of fire,
and it sat upon each of them. And they were all
filled with the Holy Ghost, and began to speak
with other tongues, as the Spirit gave them utterance.* (Acts 2:2–4)

What is the real purpose? What is God doing? Is
He giving to the individual certain powers to demonstrate and to convince the world? I do not think
that is the real reason. There is a deeper one. God
is taking possession of the inner spirit of man. From
the day that Adam sinned, the spirit of man was a
prisoner. This prison condition continues until God
releases the spirit of the individual in the baptism
of the Holy Ghost. The spirit remains dumb, unable
to express itself to mankind, until God releases the
spirit through the Holy Ghost, and the voice of the
spirit is restored.

You understand that man is a triune being—spirit, soul, and body—and these departments of human
life are very different. God manifests Himself to the
spirit of man, and the experience of real salvation is
the coming of God into the spirit of man—the infu-
sion of the spirit of man and God.

In the olden days, church leaders used to discuss
the subject of sanctification, but they were somewhat

hazy in their explanation of what it was. Sanctification is God taking possession of our mental forces, just as He took possession of our spirits when He bestowed on us eternal life. Your mind is brought into harmony with God even as your spirit was brought into harmony with God. Following the example of Jesus, we dedicate not only our spirits and souls (or minds) to God, but also our bodies to God. That is the reason we left doctors and medicine behind.

I want to talk to you about speaking in tongues by relating this experience and reciting a poem that God gave me when I was a missionary in South Africa and had my residence there. There was a dreadful epidemic of African fever, and within thirty days about one-fourth of the population of some sections of the country, both white and black, died. I was absent from my tabernacle out in the field with a group of missionaries, and we did the best we could to get them healed of God and help bury the dead.

I returned to my tabernacle after about three weeks' absence to discover that the same thing was taking place there. I was greatly distressed. My pianist was gone. My chief soloist was gone, the only daughter of an aged mother. I went to her home to console her and comfort her. As I sat by her table, she reminded me that just four weeks before, I had been present when the pianist and the soloist were practicing music in that home. My soul was very sorrowful.

As I sat meditating, I began to pray: "My God, I would like to know what sort of reception such a soul as that gets when they arrive on the other side." Presently, God spoke to my soul and said, "Take your pen and I will tell you about it."

The first thing that came was the name of the poem in tongues. Then the Lord gave me the interpretation. It was called "The Reception." Then the first verse came in tongues, and then I received from the Lord the interpretation, and then the next verses likewise, and so on. In the meantime, something transpired in my own spirit. I felt as if I was being elevated into the presence of God, and I could look down on the folks on earth, and it was described in these verses:

The Reception

List! 'Tis the morning hours in glory.
A shadow through the mists doth now appear,
A troop of angels sweeping down in greeting.
A "welcome home" rings out with joyous cheer.

A traveler from the earth is now arriving,
A mighty welcome's ringing in the skies.
The trumpets of a host are now resounding
A welcome to the life that never dies.

Who is the victor whom the angels welcome?
What mighty deeds of valor have been done?

What is the meaning of these shouts of triumph?
Why welcome this soul as a mighty one?

She is but a woman, frail and slight and tender,
No special mark of dignity she bears.
Only the Christ-light from her face doth glisten,
Only the white robe of a saint she wears.

She is but a soul redeemed by the blood of Jesus,
Hers but a life of sacrifice and care.
Yet with her welcome all the heaven is ringing,
And on her brow a victor's crown she bears.

How come she thus from sin's benighted[2] thralldom,[3]
The grace and purity of heaven to obtain?
Only through Him who gave His life a ransom,
Cleansing the soul from every spot and stain.

See! As you gaze upon her face so radiant,
'Tis but the beauty of her Lord you see.
Only the image of His life resplendent,
Only the mirror of His life is she.

See with what signs of joy they bear her onward,
How that the heavens ring with glad acclaim!
What is the shout they raise while soaring upward?
"Welcome! Thrice welcome thou in Jesus' name!"

---

[2] *benighted*: overtaken by darkness or night. *Merriam-Webster's 11th Collegiate Dictionary CD-ROM*, © 2003.

[3] *thralldom*: slavery. *Merriam-Webster's 11th Collegiate Dictionary CD-ROM*, © 2003.

Rest in the mansion the Lord prepared thee
Out of loving deeds, which thou hast done,
Furnished by thoughts and acts that portrayed He
Unto a lost world as their Christ alone.

Hear how thy lovely harp is ringing.
Touched are its strings with hands unseen.
Note the music of thine own creating
Heaven's melodies in hearts where sin has been.

See how the atmosphere with love is laden,
And that with brightness all the landscape gleams.
Know 'tis the gladness and the joy of heaven
Shed now by rescued soul in radiant beams.

Oh, that here on earth we may learn the lesson
That Christ enthroned in our hearts while here.
It fits and prepares the soul for heaven,
Making us like Him both there and here.

Doing the simple and homely duties
Just as our Christ on the earth has done,
Seeking alone that the Christ's own beauty
In every heart should be caused to bloom.

Showing all men that the blood of Jesus
Cleanses all hearts from all sin below,
And that the life of Christ within us
Transforms the soul till as pure as snow.

When we thus come to the dark, cold river,
No night, no darkness, no death is there.
Only great joy that at last the Giver
Grants us anew of His life to share.

Chapter Sixteen

The Tangible Presence of the Holy Spirit

Radio Address, Adventures in Religion #10

July 10, 1935

Today, I want to talk to you concerning one of the remarkable and outstanding incidents in the Word of God. You will find it in the nineteenth chapter of Acts. It reads:

> *And God wrought special miracles by the hands of Paul: so that from his body were brought unto the sick handkerchiefs or aprons, and the diseases departed from them, and the evil spirits went out of them.* (Acts 19:11–12)

The people brought their handkerchiefs or aprons to the apostle Paul that they might touch his person. They were then carried to the sick and laid upon them. The demons went out of them, and the sick were healed.

An examination of this incident discloses one of the most wonderful facts I know. First, that the Spirit of God is tangible. We think of the air as tangible, of electricity as tangible, and we can register the effects of them. And I want to say to you, friends, the Spirit of God is equally as tangible and can be handled and distributed, can be enclosed in a handkerchief or an apron and sent as a blessing to the one who needs it.

Get this Scripture, read it for yourself, and secure from heaven the blessing it contains. Remember that when you are in a struggle and doubts and fears assail you, God is not far away in the heavens; His Spirit is right here to bless, here to act in your life for a blessing.

Along with this line, I want to present this testimony of Mrs. Constance Hoag, who is Dean of Women at the state college in Pullman, Washington. She was visiting her son in Fairfield, Washington. They were going for a motor ride. When she stepped on the running board, her son, thinking she was already in the car, started the car. She fell and broke her kneecap, and bone protruded through the flesh. They carried her into the house, then called us on the long distance and asked that we pray and send her a handkerchief as soon as possible by messenger. We sent the handkerchief; in fifteen minutes after she received it, the bone had gone back into place. In forty-five minutes, the knee was entirely well.

However, her friends began to challenge this healing, and she found herself in the midst of a strange debate. A little later, almost the same accident happened again. She was thrown to the pavement, and the other kneecap was broken and protruded in two sections through the flesh. Once again, we prayed over a handkerchief and sent it to her, and once again the power of God acted, but this time not so quickly as the first time. The second time, she said the pain was gone in half an hour; in an hour, the bone had gone back in its place; and in an hour and a half, the knee was healed, and she was well. Friends, the Spirit of God is as tangible today as He was in the days of the apostle Paul.

Chapter Seventeen

The Spirit of Dominion and the Church

Radio Address, Adventures in Religion #11

July 11, 1935

This morning I was out on the extreme east side of the city. I ran across a strange thing. A man was coming down the street with a pack on his back. The pack was in a cowhide, which was only about half-cured. In the sack he had a cow's leg. As I came up to him, he said, "Excuse me, sir, but this is my Christian cross."

I said, "Excuse me, but it looks like just the opposite to me." He went down the street, and as far as I could hear him, he was scolding me.

Then, I went to the home of a woman who had been ill a long time. She had lain in bed and was gradually growing worse, and all the time she was accepting this sickness as from God. So I told her this foolish incident, and I said, "Dear woman, if you knew the Word of God, you would never accept a thing like that as the will of God, because Jesus most emphatically declared that sickness was not the will of God but the devil's." She had accepted that rotten, nasty business as God's will and had lain in bed for eight months.

The notion that sickness is from God is as offensive to Him as the man with his "Christian cross." Dear friends, I want you to know that the Word of God is the foundation upon which our faith is to be built.

For this purpose the Son of God was manifested, that he might destroy the works of the devil. (1 John 3:8)

God anointed Jesus of Nazareth with the Holy Ghost and with power: who went about doing good, and healing all that were **oppressed of the devil***; for God was with him.* (Acts 10:38)

You do not find "if it be Thy will" in the teaching of Jesus. He never suggested in word or deed that sin, sickness, and death were the will of God. The leper who came to Jesus for healing in the eighth chapter of Matthew did say, *"Lord, if thou wilt, thou canst make me clean."* I suppose he, too, was accepting the dirty leprosy as the will of God. Jesus instantly said, *"I will; be thou clean"* (Matthew 8:2–3). The answer of Jesus to the leper is Jesus' answer to you, to every sick man. "If it be Thy will" was never suggested in any of Jesus' teaching concerning sickness and disease. Friend, Jesus has declared His will in the most emphatic manner. His will is always to heal, if you but come to Him.

Every student of the primitive church discerns at once a distinction between the soul of the primitive

Christian and the soul of the modern Christian. It lies in the Spirit of Christ's dominion.

The Holy Spirit came into the primitive Christian soul to elevate his consciousness in Christ, to make him greater. He smote sin, and it disappeared. He cast out devils (demons); a divine flash from his Christ-nature overpowered and cast out the demon. He laid his hands on the sick, and the mighty Spirit of Jesus Christ flamed into the body, and the disease was annihilated. He was commanded to rebuke the devil, and the devil would flee from him. He was a reigning sovereign, not shrinking in fear, but overcoming by faith.

When restored to the church of Christ, it is this spirit of *dominion* that will bring again the glory-triumph to the church of God throughout the world and lift her into the place where she will become the divine instrument of God instead of being the obedient servant of the world, the flesh, and the devil. She will minister Christ's power in salvation, in healing the sick, in the casting out of demons, and in the carrying out of the whole program of Jesus' ministry, as the early church did.

Chapter Eighteen

Following the Trail of Jesus

Radio Address, Adventures in Religion #12

August 22, 1935

I want to tell you the story of an unusual family. I am going to call this story, "Following the Trail of Jesus." A number of years ago, I felt as if I wanted to do something out of the ordinary to call attention to the subject of divine healing. So, I went to the newspapers and posted $500. Then I announced that if anyone who was sick or diseased would come to the Healing Rooms and be ministered to for thirty days, he could have the $500 if, at the end of that time, he was not substantially better or healed.

Over at Monroe, Washington, was a man by the name of Paul Gering, who had gotten involved in spiritualism. That dear fellow had been an open, splendid man and a hardworking businessman. After he began dabbling in spiritualism, nobody could live with him. He was more like a raging lion than a human. He went all over the U.S., seeking deliverance from all kinds of folks who were praying for the sick.

He read my announcement and became interested. He sent me a telegram, asking me to come to Monroe, put on a meeting, and, of course, pray for him. He met Mrs. Lake and me at our hotel and drove us out to his home on the outskirts of the city. He walked into his home and stopped in the middle of the dining room and fell on his knees, saying, "Mr. Lake, I am ready for you to pray for me that I may be delivered." We laid hands on him and prayed, and bless God, the power began to go through him. He was completely delivered, the demons were cast out, and he was baptized in the Spirit. From that time on, hundreds of people have been saved and healed and baptized in the Holy Ghost under his ministry. He is now a prosperous wheat farmer in the Big Bend country.

Last night, I spent the evening at his home and conducted a public service for his relatives and neighbors. Just let me follow the trail of Jesus with you in that family for a few minutes. His sons were unsaved; his daughters were unsaved. One by one after the father's deliverance, the faith of God in his heart laid hold on God for all his family members. They became converted and baptized in the Spirit until his entire family, including his beloved wife, were saved and baptized in the Holy Ghost.

Mr. Gering had a brother, Joe, a hard fellow and a heavy drinker. He owned a farm down in the country. His wife was distressed, for she saw that he was gradually losing his grip on his affairs and squandering his money, and they were getting into financial difficulty. She was a woman of prayer and was praying for him. Finally, one day, he came to visit Paul Gering. Paul said, "Joe, I am going to Spokane to attend Mr. Lake's meeting. Come, and go with me."

We were conducting meetings in our tabernacle. When they came, we were in the prayer room. The meeting went through without anything unusual occurring, until we were practically ready to dismiss. This man, Joe Gering, was sitting on one of the back seats. A lady turned to me and asked, "Who is that man on the back seat?"

I said, "That is Paul Gering's brother."

She said, "The Lord told me to go and lay hands on him and pray, and he would be saved and baptized in the Holy Ghost."

I said, "Then you had better go do it, sister."

She went back to him and engaged him in conversation and finally asked if she might pray with him. He said he had no objection to her praying for him. So, she laid her hands on him and began to pray. As she did, the Spirit of God came down on him from heaven, and in a few minutes he yielded his heart to the Lord and prayed through until he got a real witness from heaven and began to rejoice in the Lord. After he rejoiced for a while, she said, "Now you ought to be baptized in the Holy Ghost." He knelt down again and began to pray, and after a few minutes, Joe Gering was baptized in the Holy Ghost. That man's soul was so full of rejoicing that he spent the entire night singing and praying and rejoicing and talking in tongues and sometimes in English. In a few days, he was out among the sinful and sick, getting folks saved and healed.

Here is another portion of the story. These men had a sister who lived at Palouse, Washington. She was unfortunately married to a very wicked man. She developed a tumor, and he insisted on her being operated on. She tried to tell him that the Lord always healed them in their family. He would not listen, and she was operated on. They brought her to St. Luke's Hospital in Spokane, and she was operated on. A dreadful infection developed, and they wired the family that she was going to die, so the family began to gather there to see her. I knew nothing of these circumstances.

I was riding up Monroe Street when the Spirit of the Lord said, "Go to St. Luke's Hospital and pray for Paul Gering's sister. She is dying." I went immediately and inquired at the office and was directed to her bedside. I laid my hands on her and began to pray, and the Spirit of the Lord came upon the woman. The infection was destroyed, and in ten minutes she was sound asleep, and the next day was on the highway to a blessed recovery. These are some of the things that take place when folks get in line with God.

Their old mother was a godly woman who lived at Palouse. She had been notified that her daughter was ready to die. When she got the word, she went into her closet and interceded with God and prayed for the daughter's deliverance. I believe before God that when God spoke to me, it was the answer to that mother's prayer. He sent help through me, and the Lord made her whole.

GERBER GIRL'S HEALING

One day, Mrs. Lake and I were present in a gathering of Christian people where these Gering people were meeting with some of their neighbors. A family by the name of Gerber had a girl seventeen or eighteen years old. She stood up with her back to us, and I remarked to Mrs. Lake, "Did you ever see such a perfect form? That girl would do for an artist's model." But when she turned around, I was shocked at her appearance. I never saw anyone so cross-eyed. She was a dreadful sight.

Later, I talked to the father, and he told me that surgeons would not undertake to straighten her eyes. They said it was impossible, and if they undertook it, she was likely to lose her eyesight. Presently, the young girl came over our way, and I said, "Sit down, little woman. I want to talk to you." After talking a few minutes, I stood up and laid my hands on her eyes. The Spirit of God came upon her, and those eyes were as straight as they were supposed to be in three minutes' time.

She is now married and has a beautiful home and lovely babies. Her eyes and heart are straight.

Chapter Nineteen

The Baptism of the Holy Ghost

Sermon

Chicago Pentecostal Convention • July 16, 1920

There are as many degrees in God in the baptism of the Holy Ghost as there are preachers who preach it. Some people are born way down, weeping at the feet of the cross. They are still on the earth-plane with Christ. They are still weeping over their sins, still trying to overcome sin and be pure of heart.

But there are other people who are born way up in the blessed dominion of God, like our Mother Etter. They have resurrection power. All power is given, and it is in our soul.

And, beloved, one day there are going to be Christians baptized in the Holy Ghost who are way up in the throne room of God, way up in the consciousness that is breathed out of His holy heart. Somebody is going to be born a son of God and be baptized in the Holy Ghost where Jesus is today, in the throne-consciousness of Christ; where he can say like Jesus said, where he can feel like Jesus feels: *"I am he that liveth, and was dead; and, behold, I am alive for evermore, Amen; and have the keys of hell and of death*" (Revelation 1:18). Absolute overcoming consciousness!

You dear folks, listen, who are trying to pump up a Pentecost that was worn out years ago. God let it die. God had only one way under heaven to get you to move up into God, and that way is to let you become dissatisfied with the thing you have. And if you have not the consciousness you once had, God Almighty understands the situation. He is trying to get you hungry, so that you will commit your body and your soul and your spirit to God forever; and by the grace of God, you will be baptized in the Holy Ghost again at the throne of God-consciousness, in the power of Jesus Christ, as Jesus is today: "*As he is, so are we in this world*" (1 John 4:17).

Why, with most of you, when you were baptized in the Holy Ghost, the Lord had to baptize a whole dose of medicine and pills and everything that was in you. Well, God never had to baptize that kind of stuff in the Lord Jesus. Jesus came down to the River Jordan and gave His *body* and His *soul* and His *spirit* to God forever, and He never took a pill or a dose of medicine. He never went to the spirit of the world for assistance or to the devil for help. His spirit, His soul, and His body were God's from that minute, forever.

Beloved, God is calling men and women to a holier consecration, to a higher place in God, and I am one of

God's candidates for that holy place in God. I want to get to the throne of God. Oh, yes, God baptized me in the Holy Ghost with a wondrous baptism, according to the understanding I possessed ten or fifteen years ago. But I am a candidate today for a new baptism in the Holy Ghost that comes out of the heart of the *glorified* Christ in the lightnings of God, everlasting overcoming on the throne with Jesus.

And that is the experience that is going to make the sons of God in the world. That is the reason they will take the world for Jesus Christ, and the kingdom will be established, and they will put the crown on the Son of God and declare Him *"King of kings, and Lord of lords"* (1 Timothy 6:15; Revelation 19:16) forever. Amen.

Interpretation of a Message in Tongues

Therefore, fear not, for God is able to perform in you even that which He performed in Jesus and raise you likewise in union with Christ Jesus and make you reign in dominion over sin instead of being dominated by the powers of evil and darkness.

Chapter Twenty

The Calling of the Soul

Sermon

Spokane, Washington • March 6, 1916

Blessed are they which do hunger and thirst after righteousness: for they shall be filled.
                                    (Matthew 5:6)

Someone has given us this little saying that has become prevalent among many people: "My own shall come to me." Jesus framed that thought in different words. He said, "He who hungers and thirsts after righteousness shall be filled." It is the same law. *"Blessed are they which do hunger and thirst after righteousness: for they shall be filled"* (Matthew 5:6).

Righteousness is simply God's rightness—God's rightness in a man's soul, God's rightness in a man's spirit, God's rightness in a man's body. In order that man may be right, or righteous, God imparts to man the power of His Spirit. The Holy Spirit contains such marvelous and transforming grace that, when it is received into the nature of man, the marvelous process of regeneration is set in motion, and man becomes thereby a new creature in Christ Jesus.

The deepest call of our nature is the one that will find the speediest answer. People pray; something happens. If they pray again, something still deeper occurs within their nature, they find a new level of prayer, and the desire is obtained. (See James 5:16.)

In my ministry in South Africa, I had a preacher by the name of Van Vuuren. That name means "fire." Van Vuuren had been a butcher in the city of Johannesburg and was given up to die of consumption.[4] His physician said to him, "You have only one year to live." So, he gave up his business and went out into the country to develop a farm with the intent that his family might be able to support themselves.

After he left the city, many were baptized in the Holy Spirit and healed, etc., and his friends wrote him a letter and said, "So-and-so, who was sick, has been healed. So-and-so, your niece, has been baptized in the Holy Spirit and is speaking in tongues by the power of God. So-and-so has been blessed of God," etc.

Van Vuuren took the letter, went out into the fields, got down under a thorn tree, and spread the letter out before God. Then he began to pray, "God, if You can do these things for the people at Johannesburg, You can do something for me. I have been a Christian for eighteen years, and I have prayed and prayed for certain things which have not come to pass. God, if others can be baptized in the Holy Ghost, surely I can. If others' hearts are made pure by Your power, the power that

---

[4] *consumption*: a progressive wasting away of the body, especially from tuberculosis. *Merriam-Webster's 11th Collegiate Dictionary* CD-ROM, © 2003.

made theirs pure can make mine pure also. If others have been healed, then You can heal me."

As he thus gave himself to God and opened his soul to heaven, suddenly the Spirit came upon him, and he became the most transformed creature I ever knew. God moved in the man. For eighteen days, he walked as though overshadowed by the Spirit of God; God talked continuously to his soul, directing him to this person and that one, judges and lawyers, statesmen and physicians, rich and poor. When he would meet them, the Spirit of God would pour forth through his soul such messages that, in many cases, they fell down and wept.

This is the point of the story I wanted you to get. He said for eighteen years he had prayed for the real conversion and transformation of his wife, and it had not come to pass. But that morning, after the Lord had baptized him in the Holy Ghost, a new prayer came into his heart. A new depth had been touched in the man's nature, and from that great inner depth flowed out to God a cry that had been going out from his soul for years. But that morning, the groaning of the Holy Spirit from deep within him (see Romans 8:26) touched the soul of his wife. Before he reached the house, she had given her heart to God. In three months all his family—his wife and eleven children, as well as himself—had been baptized in the Holy Spirit.

THE HUNGER OF THE SOUL

The hunger of which Jesus spoke when He said, *"Blessed are they which do hunger and thirst after righteousness: for they shall be filled,"* is this same desire, this call of the soul, which is not the simple attitude of the outer, natural man. Certainly, it includes it, and perhaps the original desire in the beginning may simply be that of the mind. However, when the desirability of becoming more Christlike grows in the soul as the days and years pass, it becomes a call of the deepest depths of a person's nature. And that is the character of desire of which Jesus spoke.

The spiritual action that takes place within the nature of man, that strong yearning for God—His ways, His love, His knowledge, His power—causes everything else, perhaps unconsciously to the person, to become secondary.

PARAMOUNT HEART ISSUES

Politicians talk about a paramount issue—the issue that stands out by itself above all others and is the greatest and largest and of most interest to the nation. It is the paramount issue.

The soul also has its paramount issue. When the desire of your heart is intensified so that it absorbs all your energies, then the time of its fulfillment is not far away. That is the desire that brings the answer. It is creative desire.

A woman testified in my hearing one day to this fact. She had been pronounced hopeless and was going blind. No human remedy could do her any good. Someone opened to her, in a dim way, the possibility of her seeing through the power of God. She was not very well-taught, but she said this: "Every day for four years, I spent two and a half hours absolutely expressing the desire of my soul for real sight." Not only expressing it in words, but calling the power of God to her that would re-create in her the function of sight in her eyes and make her see. At the end of four and a half years, she said, "My eyes are as well as they ever were."

That is the reward of persistence of a desire toward God. Your nature may have sent out just as deep a cry to God as my nature has and still is doing. Is your cry to God continuous? Gradually, as the forces of life concentrate themselves in line with that strong desire, the Spirit of God is operating through your heart, is being directed by that desire and concentrated on a particular line, intensifying every day because of your continuous desire to possess your heart's desire. The effect of that concentration of the Spirit of God on your soul is that, by the grace of God, there is brought to you all the elements necessary to formulate and create and fulfill the desire of your heart. And one morning, you awaken to discover that you have become the possessor of the desired object.

FIRST SEEK RIGHTEOUSNESS

Jesus started men on the true foundation. Many simply desire health; others temporal blessings. Both are good and proper, but bless God, Jesus started the soul at the proper point: to first desire righteousness, the righteousness of God, in order to become a possessor of the kingdom. Jesus said, *"Seek ye first the kingdom of God, and his righteousness; and all these things shall be added unto you"* (Matthew 6:33).

Jesus was bringing forth and establishing in the world a new character, a character that would endure forever, a soul quality that would never fail, a faith that knew no possibility of defeat. In establishing such a character, Jesus saw that the character could be established only in the depth of a man's being, in the very spirit of his being. Then, when once the soul was grounded in the paths of righteousness, all the activities of the nature would be along righteous lines and in harmony with the laws of God.

God has a call in His own Spirit. If we study our spirits, we will understand the nature of God. The call of the Spirit of God is the call of righteousness, the call of truth, the call of love, the call of power, the call of faith.

I met a young man on one occasion who seemed to me to be the most blessed man, in some ways, of all the men I had ever met. I observed he was surrounded by a circle of friends of men and women, the deepest and truest it had ever been my privilege to know. One day I said to him, "What is the secret of this circle of friends that you possess and the manner in which you seem to bind them to you?" He replied, "Lake, my friendships are the result of the call of the soul. My soul has called for truth and righteousness, for holiness, for grace, for strength, for soundness of mind, for the power of God; and the call has reached this one, and that one, and this one, and brought them to me."

Over in Topeka, Kansas, one morning in the year 1900, a man stepped off the train and walked up the street. As he walked up a particular street, he stopped in front of a large, fine dwelling and said to himself, "This is the house." A gentleman happened to be out of sight around the building, but within earshot. When he asked, "What about the house?" this story came out.

The newcomer said, "For years, I have been praying God for a certain work of God among Christians known as the baptism of the Holy Ghost. In my research, I have visited every body of Christian people in this country that I knew of that claimed to be possessors of the baptism. However, as I visited and examined their experiences and compared each with the Word of God, I became convinced that none of them possesses the baptism of the Holy Ghost as it is recorded and demonstrated in the New Testament."

He said that one day as he prayed, the Spirit of the Lord said, "Go to Topeka, Kansas." As he prayed, he observed in the Spirit a certain house, and the Lord said, "I will give you that house, and in it the baptism of the Holy Ghost will fall."

So he took the train and came to Topeka, walked down the street, and exclaimed as he passed by, "This is the house."

And the voice around the corner replied, "What about it?" When the man had heard his story, he told him he was the owner of the house, that it had been closed up for years. He asked him what he wanted it for, and he replied that he was going to start a Christian school. The owner said, "Have you any money?"

He replied, "No."

He said, "All right, you can have the house without money."

About an hour later, a little Quaker lady came down the street, hesitated, looked around, and said, "This is the house, but there is no one living there." After a struggle with her soul, she went up and rang the doorbell, and the first gentleman answered the

119

bell and asked what she wanted. She said, "I live over in the country at such-and-such a place. As I prayed, the Spirit told me to come here to this house."

He said, "Who are you?"

She replied, "Just an unknown Christian woman."

He said, "What have you been praying about?"

She said, "About the baptism of the Holy Ghost."

Beloved, in three weeks, eighteen people were brought to that house. They formed a little group and began to pray. The company grew to thirty-six. On New Year's night, 1900, the Spirit fell on that company, and the first one was baptized in the Holy Ghost. In a few weeks, practically the whole company had been baptized in the Holy Ghost. And from there it spread over the world.

Yesterday morning, a woman came to my healing rooms, a stranger in the city. She said, "I have been praying for healing and asking God to show me where I could be healed. I heard of friends in Chicago who pray for the sick, and I visited them, but when I arrived the Spirit said, 'Not here.'"

She said, "I bought a ticket and was about to take a train back home, but as I sat in the station, I was approached by a little lady on crutches. Pitying her, I turned to speak a kind word to her. While conversing with her, I saw she was a Christian of a deep nature that is rarely found. I told her my story. She said, 'Oh,

I know where the Lord wants you to go; He wants you to go to Spokane, Washington.'" (Spokane is three thousand miles from Chicago.)

She asked her if she knew anybody in Spokane, and the lady replied, "Why, yes, I know Mr. Lake. I used to nurse in his home years ago."

The woman arrived here yesterday and sought me out. I prayed for her and told her the thing to do was to come in for ministry every day until she was well. She said she would. This morning, I received a call on the telephone, and she said, "I am not coming up to the healing rooms."

I said, "Oh, is that the kind of individual you are— the one who comes once and gets nothing?"

"No," she said, "I came once and got something, and I do not need to come back. I am healed, and I am going home."

There is a call of faith in this church that is reaching way out, far out, in unaccountable ways. Way at the other end of that call of faith, the Spirit of God is revealing truth to this soul and that soul, and they are moving into this life and coming into unity with this church.

Is there a note of despair in your heart? Have you not attained the thing your soul covets? Have you desired to be like that sinless, unselfish, healthy one? God will answer the call of your soul. You shall have your heart's desire. But before that call becomes answerable, it must be the paramount call of your being. It is when it becomes the paramount issue of the soul that the answer comes. Jesus knew. That is the reason He said, *"Blessed are they which do hunger and thirst after righteousness: for they shall be filled."*

There is not a doubt about it. All the barriers of your nature will break down before the desire of the soul. All the obstacles that ever were will disappear before the desire of your soul. All the diseases that ever existed in your life will disappear before the desire of your soul when that desire becomes the one great purpose and prayer of your heart.

I love to think of one great soul. He was not a great Christian, but he was a great soul. He was the son of a Church of England clergyman and came to South Africa thinking he might get himself back to a normal state of health. He came to the diamond mines at Kimberly and took a pick and a shovel and worked with them long enough to understand diamonds. Indeed, he studied diamonds until he knew more about them than any other man in the world. Then he went to studying Africa until one paramount desire grew up in his soul. He said, "I will plant the British flag across the continent." Eventually, this is what he did. He told me that in the beginning his vision extended to the Vaal River, then to the Zambezi, and then across the trackless desert. He also planned a railroad six thousand miles long. John Cecil Rhodes died before he could fully bring to pass the paramount issue of his soul.

"Blessed are they which do hunger and thirst after righteousness." Oh, if I had one gift or one desire that I could bestow on you more than all others, I would bestow upon you the hunger for God.

"Blessed are they which do hunger." Hunger is the best thing that ever came into a man's life. Hunger is hard to endure. It is the call of your nature for something that you do not possess. The thing that will satisfy the demands of hunger in a man's soul is the call of his nature for the Spirit of life that will generate in him the abundant love of God.

Years ago, I was one of a family of which some member or another was an invalid in the house for thirty-two consecutive years. During that time, we buried four brothers and four sisters. A call arose in my nature to God for something to stay that tide of sickness and death. *Materia Medica*[5] had utterly failed. One after another the tombstones were raised.

The call arose in my soul for something from God that would stem the tide and turn it backward. Nothing else but healing could have come to my life,

---

[5] *Materia Medica*: a treatise on materia medica, the substances used in the composition of medical remedies; a branch of medical science that deals with the sources, nature, properties, and preparation of drugs. *Merriam-Webster's 11th Collegiate Dictionary* CD-ROM, © 2003.

no other thing but the knowledge of it. God had to bring, from the furthest ends of Australia, the man (John Alexander Dowie) who brought to my soul the message of God and the manifestation of His power that satisfied my heart. And through him, healing by the power of God became a fact to me.

We live in order that our souls may grow. The development of the soul is the purpose of existence. God Almighty is trying to obtain some decent association for Himself. By His grace, He is endeavoring to have us grow up in His knowledge and likeness to that stature (see Ephesians 4:13–15) where, as sons of God, we will comprehend something of His love, of His nature, of His power, of His purpose, and be big enough to give back to God what a son should give to a great Father—the reverence, the love, the affection that comes from the understanding of the nobleness and greatness of His purpose.

Great Britain produced two marvelous statesmen, a father and his son. They were known in history as William Pitt, the Elder, and William Pitt, the Younger. The young Pitt was as great a statesman as his father. The son grew to that place where, catching the vision of his great father, his soul arose to it, and he became his father's equal. As I walked through the House of Commons, I came across the statues of the old and young Pitt. I have forgotten the inscription at the bottom of the elder Pitt's statue, but at the base of the son's statue were these words: "My father, the greatest man I ever knew." Do you see the call of his soul for his father's largeness, for his father's nobility, for his father's strength and influence?

"Blessed are they which do hunger." What are we hungering for, a little bit of God, just enough to take us through this old world where we will have dry rot and be stunted and then squeeze into heaven? *"Blessed are they which do hunger"* for the nature and power and love and understanding of God. Why? *"For they shall be filled."* Bless God!

Not long ago, I stood before great audiences of the churchmen of the world. They said, "Throughout your entire ministry, there is one note. It is the call for power." They said, "Do you not think it would be better if the church was calling for holiness instead of power?"

And I replied, "She will never obtain the one without the other. There is something larger than holiness. It is the nature of God."

The nature of God has many sides. From every angle that the soul approaches God, it reveals a new and different manifestation of Him: love, beauty, tenderness, healing, power, might, wisdom, etc.

So the Christian who hungers and hungers, bless God, and lifts his soul to God, brings God down to meet his own cry. The spirit of man and the Spirit of

God unite. The nature of God is reproduced in man, as God purposed it should be. There are no sick folk in God. There is no sickness in His nature.

There is an incident in the life of Jesus that is so marvelous. Jesus Christ demanded His right to heal a woman who was so bound by Satan with a spirit of infirmity and was not satisfied until it was accomplished. Devil and church and creed and preacher backed down before the call of the Son of God to assert His right to deliver that soul from sin and sickness. *"Blessed are they which do hunger."*

Chapter Twenty-one

Christian Consciousness

Sermon

Chicago, Illinois • July 16, 1920

God's purpose—and the purpose of real Christianity—is to create in man's nature a consciousness of God. The word *consciousness*, as I am using it, means "that which the soul knows"—not what you believe or what you have faith for or what you hope for, but what the soul has proven, what the soul knows, upon which the soul rests—what has become concrete in your life. The church that succeeds in creating the highest degree of consciousness of God in the soul of man will live longest in the world. Further, the only mode of possibility of perpetuating a church in the world forever is to bring into the souls of the people the full measure of the consciousness of God that Jesus Christ enjoys. It is a good thing not only to be good, but also to know why you are good. It is a good thing not only to be an American, but also to know why you are an American. It is a good thing not only to be a Christian, but also to know why you are a Christian, and to know why Christian consciousness is superior to every other known consciousness.

Today, I want to declare that Christianity stands superior to every other form of religion under the heavens and in the whole earth, because no other religion under the heavens has the same consciousness of God or the same means of producing a consciousness of God that Christianity possesses.

In 1893, the great World's Fair was held here in Chicago. Among the features of the fair was a Congress on Religions. All the religions of the world were invited to send their representatives and present their particular religion for the good of all. Many regarded it as a great calamity that the varied forms of Eastern philosophy should thus be introduced into this country. I never felt that way. I have always felt that if Christianity could not demonstrate her superiority over every other religion, then Christianity does not have the place and power that Jesus Christ said Christianity has in the world.

However, the result of that Congress of Religions was that Christianity was so poorly presented that the Indian philosophers ran away with the whole thing. In the minds of thousands who listened, a distinct impression was made that the Indian philosophers' knowledge of God and God's laws and the laws of life were greater than what the Christian possessed.

Fellow Christians, at that time there began in my soul a prayer that God Almighty would reveal in my soul what the real secret of real Christianity is, in order that in this world Christians might become kings and priests (see Revelation 5:10) and demonstrate the superiority of the religion of the Son of God beyond that of every other in the whole earth.

In later years, I went to South Africa. It was at a time of peculiar interest in South African history, just following the Boer War. The great industry there is mining. One-fourth of the gold of the world comes from the vicinity of Johannesburg, South Africa. Most of the diamonds of the world also come from South Africa, and the United States is the greatest diamond market of the world.

When the Boer War started, the native people became so frightened over war between white men that, after the war was over and settled, they could not coax them back to open the mines. The result was that in order to get the industries established again, they had to send to China for 200,000 Chinese and put them to work to open the shops and mines and all the other industries. These Chinese came in real colonies. Some were Confucians, some were Buddhists, some were Brahmans, some represented this form of philosophy, and some that form. They brought their priests, and their priests ministered to them.

At the same time, there were in South Africa one and a half million East Indians. These represented all the cults of India. They made complaint that they were not being properly cared for, and the British government sent to India and imported a great company of Buddhist priests and Brahman priests and Yogi priests and all the rest of them, and they came to South Africa to assist their own people.

I had a Jewish friend, Rabbi Hertz, who became famous as a great rabbi because of his influence for the British during the war. There was also a Roman Catholic priest, Father Bryant, a wonderful man. I listened to Dr. Hertz give a series of lectures on the psalms of David, which I regard as the finest I had ever heard.

One day he said, "Did it ever occur to you what an amazing Congress of Religions we have in this country? It would put the one in Chicago in 1893 to shame."

I said, "I have thought of it but do not have sufficient acquaintance among these other men to undertake it, but I would gladly give a helping hand." So it was eventually brought to pass.

We gathered once a week. They sat on the floor all night, Eastern fashion, a priest with his interpreter. We gave the individual a whole night if he wanted it, or two nights, or as long as he wanted to tell out the very secrets of his soul, to show the very best he could the very depth of his peculiar religion and the consciousness of God it produced. It was not the details of his religion we sought, but the soul of it and the consciousness it possessed.

We listened to the Indian Buddhist priest one night and the Chinese Buddhist priest the next night; the Indian Confucian priest one night and the Chinese Confucian priest the next night; the Indian Brahman priest one night and a Chinese Brahman priest the next night; and on it went. Eventually, it came to the night that Dr. Hertz, the Jewish rabbi, was to give the secret of the Jewish religion and tell out the whole of God that the Jewish religion revealed and the consciousness of God that was produced by the Mosaic and the prophetic teachings.

Did you ever stop to think that, in all religious history, the Jewish prophets knew more of God than all the philosophers of earth combined? They superseded all others of the ancients in their knowledge of God, His ways, and His power. They gave to their day and generation such a revelation of God as the world had ever known. Stop and think of the wonders of God that the Old Testament revealed. Think of the marvels that it seems would stagger the very soul of modern Christianity.

When the Israelites were traveling over the desert, God stopped the process of decay from their very shoes and clothing, and they wore them continually for forty years. (See Deuteronomy 8:4.) Think of the marvel of it, the halting of the process of decay! And then someone wonders if it is possible to halt the process of decay in a man's life. Yes, it is, bless God! Jesus Christ stops the process of spiritual death by the power of God, through the introduction of the life in Jesus Christ and the Spirit of life, giving man eternal life.

Think of the prophet Elisha. When the sons of the prophets had lost the ax head in the water and came to him in their distress, Elisha cut down a stick and held it in his hands. And when he threw it in the water, the ax arose. (See 2 Kings 6:1–6.)

Later, after Elisha had died and was buried, some Israelites were burying another man, but in their haste they opened the grave of Elisha and put the man's body in with Elisha. When the dead man touched Elisha's God-filled bones, he revived. (See 2 Kings 13:21.) There was enough of God in Elisha's old bones to quicken the man unto life again. Bless God.

You say, "Well, how can Christianity demonstrate anything further than that?" When I listened to Dr. Hertz, my heart asked: "Dear God, when I get my turn to reveal what Christianity is, what am I going to say that is going to reveal Christianity as superior to the Jewish dispensations and the consciousness of God that it produced in the souls of the prophet?"

From eight o'clock at night until 4:30 the next morning, Dr. Hertz poured out his soul in a wondrous stream of God-revelation such as my soul had never heard before. As I started for home, I prayed, "God, in the name of Jesus, when it comes next Thursday night and it is my turn to show forth Jesus Christ, what am I going to say to surmount the revelation of God that he gave?"

I searched Christian literature for it. I could not find it in the writings of the old Christian fathers. I searched the Word of God for it. I saw flashes of it, but somehow it would not frame in my soul. I decided there was only one way. I gave myself to fasting and prayer and waiting on God.

And one day, in the quiet, God told me the secret. From that day, my heart rested in the new vision of Jesus Christ, and a new revelation of the real divinity of Christianity came to my heart.

So it came my turn, and I sat down and reviewed for hours with care, step by step, the consciousness that the philosophers and priests had shown as belonging to their respective religions, and finally the wonderful consciousness that Dr. Hertz had shown as belonging to the Mosaic dispensation.

Oh, bless God, there is a secret in Jesus Christ. Christianity is all supernatural, every bit of it. The philosophies are natural. The Mosaic dispensation and its revelation was supernatural, but its revelation did not have the high degree of overcoming consciousness that belongs to Christianity. Yet you can go around the world, and you will not find one in a hundred thousand that can tell what the real secret of Christianity is that makes it superior to all other religions.

You say, "It is the Holy Ghost." Well, the prophets had the Holy Ghost. There is the marvelous account given in the Old Testament records. When Moses needed laborers and workmen for the new tabernacle, the Lord appointed certain skilled workmen to carry out the construction:

See, I have called by name Bezaleel the son of Uri, the son of Hur, of the tribe of Judah: I have filled him with the spirit of God, in wisdom, and in understanding, and in knowledge, and in all manner of workmanship, to devise cunning works, to work in gold, and in silver, and in brass, and in cutting of stones, to set them, and in carving of timber, to work all manner of workmanship. And I, behold, I have given with him Aholiab, the son of Ahisamach, of the tribe of Dan: and in the hearts of all that are wise hearted I have put wisdom, that they may make all that I have commanded thee.

(Exodus 31:2–6)

That is the way they learned their trade.

Later, they were making preparations for the building of Solomon's temple. Did you ever stop to think of where the plans came from or how they got them? David tells us that God gave him the plans of the temple in writing: *"All this,...the Lord made me understand in writing by his hand upon me, even all the works* [details] *of this pattern"* (1 Chronicles 28:19). He put these details down with such accuracy that they prepared the temple in the mountains, and when they came to put it together on the temple site, there was no sound of a hammer. (See 1 Kings 6:7.) Every piece fit to piece.

What a wonderful moving of God! Wonderful presence of God! Talk about the glory of God. Why, when Moses came down from the mountain, his face shone or radiated with the glory of God so intensely, the people were afraid of him, and he was compelled to wear a veil until the anointing had somewhat left his soul. (See Exodus 34:29–35.)

But, beloved, Christianity is more than that. Paul declared that the glory of Moses' face was superseded. I said a moment ago that Christianity is not a natural religion. It has nothing natural in it. It is *supernatural* from the top to the bottom, from the center to the circumference, within and without. It comes right from heaven, every bit of it. It is the divine outflow of the holy soul of the crucified, risen, glorified Son of God.

Why does God come down from heaven into the hearts of men, into the natures of men, into the bodies

135

of men, into the souls of men, into the spirits of men? God's purpose in man is to transform him into the nature of God.

The philosophers came to the grave and died. They had no further revelation to give. They had left their tenets, and they exist to this day. I have studied the great eastern philosophies. I have searched them from cover to cover. I have read them for years as diligently as I have read my Bible. I have read them to see what their consciousness was. The secret of salvation is not in them.

But, in my Bible is seen that the Son of God saves men from their sins and changes them by His power in their nature so that they become like Him. And that is the purpose of Jesus: to take a man and make him thoroughly Christlike. To take a sinner and wash him pure and white and clean, and then come into his life and anoint him with His Spirit, speak through him, live in him, change the substance of his spirit, change the substance of his body—until his body and his blood and his bones and his flesh and his soul and his spirit are the body and blood and bones and flesh and soul and spirit of the Son of God. (See Ephesians 5:30 and 1 Corinthians 6:17.)

Oh, Jesus was crucified. Jesus was crucified after there grew in His soul the divine consciousness that He could go into the grave and, through faith in God, accept the Word of God and believe that He would raise Him from the dead. Jesus went into the grave with a divine boldness, not simply as a martyr. He was God's Prince, God's King, God's Savior. He went into the grave as God's Conqueror. He was after something. He went after the power of death, and He got it. He took it captive, and He came forth from the grave proclaiming His victory over death.

No more bowing before the accursed power that had been generated through sin. It was a captive. No more fear of hell! Do you hear it? No more fear of hell after Jesus Christ came out of the grave. He had death and hell by the throat and the key in His hands. He was Conqueror!

When He came forth from the grave, He came forth bringing that wonderful Spirit of heavenly triumph that was begotten in the soul of Jesus because He had not failed. He had gone and done it! No longer was it a *hope*, no longer a *faith*, now a *knowledge*— God's consciousness in His heart. It was done!

Oh, bless God, I am coming back to that word with which I started. Do you know the secret of religion is in its consciousness? The secret of Christianity is in the consciousness it produces in your soul—and Christianity produces a higher consciousness than any other religion in the world. No other religion in the world or other revelation of the true God equals

137

it. It is the highest and holiest. It comes breathing and throbbing and burning, right out of the heart of the glorified Son of God. It comes breathing and beating and burning and throbbing into your nature and mine, bless God.

So, that is the reason I love the religion of the Lord and Savior Jesus Christ. That is the reason the cross of Calvary is a sacred place. That is the reason that the conquest of the Son of God in the regions of death makes a man's heart throb. That is the reason He gathered His disciples together and, as if He could not wait, said, "Let Me breathe My Spirit into you. Go forth in My power. All power is given unto Me, both in heaven and in earth. Go ye therefore. These signs shall follow you: cast out devils, speak with new tongues, heal the sick." (See John 20:22; Matthew 28:18–19; Mark 16:17–18.) Amen.

In those early centuries of Christianity, Christians did not go into the world apologizing. They went to slay the powers of darkness and undo the works of the devil, and they lived in holy triumph.

HEALING CONSCIOUSNESS

When you see those holy flashes of heavenly flame once in awhile in a person's life, as we observe in our Sister Etter when someone is healed, it is because her consciousness and Christ's are one. She is fused into God. I saw a dying, strangling woman healed in thirty seconds as Mrs. Etter cast out a demon. The flame of God, the fire of His Spirit, ten seconds of connection with Christ Almighty at the throne of God—that is the secret of it.

Oh, I would like to get you in touch with the Son of God for five minutes. I would like to see the streams of God's lightning come down for ten minutes! I wonder what would take place.

A few months ago, I was absent from the city of Spokane, and when I returned, we discovered Mrs. Lake was not at home. It was just time to leave for my afternoon service. Just then, someone came in and said, "Your secretary, Mrs. Graham, is in the throes of death, and your wife is with her." So I hurried down to the place. When I got there, the wife of one of my ministers met me at the door and said, "You are too late; she has gone." And as I stepped in, I met the minister coming out of the room, who said, "She has not breathed for a long time." But my heart flamed as I looked down at that woman and thought of how God Almighty, three years before, had raised her out of death. After her womb and ovaries and tubes had been removed in operations, God Almighty had given them back to her, after which she had married and conceived. I took that woman up off that pillow and called on God for the lightning of heaven to blast the power of death and deliver her. I commanded her to come back and stay, and she came back, after not breathing for twenty-three minutes.

We have not yet learned to keep in touch with the powers of God. Once in a while our souls rise, and we see the flame of God accomplish this wonder and that. But beloved, Jesus Christ lived in the presence of God every hour of the day and night. Never a word proceeded from the mouth of Jesus Christ but what was God's Word. *"The words that I speak unto you, they are spirit, and they are life"* (John 6:63). When you and I are lost in the Son of God, and the fires of Jesus burn in our hearts like they did in Him, our words will be the words of life and of spirit, and there will be no death in them. But, beloved, we are on the way.

I have read church and religious history because my heart was searching for the truth of God. I have witnessed with my own eyes the most amazing manifestation of psychological power. I knew an East Indian Yogi who volunteered to be buried for three days, and he came up out of the grave well and whole. I saw them put a man in a cataleptic state, place a stone fifteen inches square on his body, put his feet on one chair and his head on another, and strike that stone with a twenty-five pound sledgehammer seven times, until it broke in two.

I watched these things, and I said, "These are only on the psychological plane. Beyond that is the spirit plane and the amazing wonder of the Holy Spirit of God. If God got hold of my spirit for ten minutes, He could do something ten thousand times greater than that."

Why, Jesus was the triumphant One. Did you ever stop to think of Jesus at the throne of God? I like to think of the twentieth-century Christ, not the Jesus who lived in the world two thousand years ago, not the humiliated Jesus, not Jesus dying on the cross for my sin. Instead, I like to dwell on the glorified, exalted Son of God at the throne of God who stands declaring, *"I am he that liveth, and was dead; and, behold, I am alive for evermore, Amen; and have the keys of hell and of death"* (Revelation 1:18). Blessed be God.

That is the Christ that breathes His power into your soul and mine. That is the consciousness that is breathed from heaven in the Holy Ghost when it comes to your heart. Amen.

God purposed that the Christian church should be the embodiment of the living, blessed Son of God—the Spirit of Christ living not in one temple (Jesus), but in multitudes of temples. The bodies of those yielded to God in holy consecration, God's real church, not in name only but in power. Many members, yet one in spirit, one divine structure of divine faith and substance—man transformed, transfigured, and transmuted into the nature, the glory, and the substance of Christ.

THE EVIL ONE CAN'T TOUCH A SEPARATED MAN

We know that whosoever is born of God sinneth not; but he that is begotten of God keepeth himself, and that wicked one toucheth him not.

(1 John 5:18)

When the Spirit of God radiated from the man Jesus, how close to Him do you suppose it was possible for the devil to come? I believe it was impossible for any evil spirit to come anywhere near Him. The Spirit of God is as destructive of evil as it is creative of good. I am sure that Satan talked to Jesus from a safe distance.

The real Christian is a *separated* man. He is separated forever unto God in *all* the departments of his life. Thus, his body and his soul and his spirit are forever committed to the Father. From the time he commits himself to God, his body is as absolutely in the hands of God as his spirit or his soul. He can go to no other power for help or healing. A hundredfold consecration takes the individual forever out of the hands of all but God.

Chapter Twenty-two

Consciousness of God

Sermon

November 26, 1916

And when the day of Pentecost was fully come, they were all with one accord in one place. And suddenly there came a sound from heaven as of a rushing mighty wind, and it filled all the house where they were sitting. And there appeared unto them cloven tongues like as of fire, and it sat upon each of them. And they were all filled with the Holy Ghost, and began to speak with other tongues, as the Spirit gave them utterance. (Acts 2:1–4)

On the day of Pentecost, the hundred and twenty who composed the little circle of believers that had met in the upper room after the ascension of Jesus were sitting together in prayer and meditation upon God. Suddenly there came from heaven—not born out of man's emotionalism, but by faith—there came from heaven the sound of a rushing, mighty wind, and it filled the house where they were sitting. And there appeared cloven tongues like fire, which rested upon each of them, and they were filled with the Holy Ghost, the living Spirit of God. As a result of being thus filled, they began to speak with other tongues as the Spirit gave them utterance. That filling of the Holy Ghost, that coming of the living Spirit of Jesus Christ upon mankind, was the dawning morning of the first Christian day. That was the day-dawn of Christianity. Christianity never existed before. Religion existed, but Christianity never existed before. The Christianity of Christ has its birth then and there, bless God. It had not even manifested itself in the world during Jesus' own lifetime nor during the forty days after His resurrection.

Christianity has a secret, bless God, the secret of divine power, the secret that makes it different from other known religions. It is the secret of the consciousness that it contains, and the consciousness that Christianity contains is due to the fact that the Spirit of the triumphant Son of God, who had entered into death, who had experienced resurrection and thereby power over death, who had ascended in triumph to the right hand of God and sat down a victor, was poured forth upon the world. He poured forth His own living Spirit, containing that consciousness. Consequently, when the Spirit of Christ came upon the disciples on the day of Pentecost, it produced in them, of necessity, that which was in the mind of Christ, the same consciousness of power and victory and dominion and Christlikeness that was common to the nature of Jesus Himself as He sat down in triumph at God's right hand.

When I went to Africa and sat down quietly to study the native peoples and their minds, I was forced to study myself and my people, too. I said, "What is the thing that makes us Anglo-Saxons different from these native people?"

My friend said, "Well, it is our education."

I said, "Education does not do it."

He said, "Yes, it does."

I said, "No, it doesn't. I will show you why."

And I took him down to one of the towns and introduced him to an educated native missionary. Some missionaries had sent him over here, and he was educated at Yale, and he was just as much a heathen as he ever was. He was an educated heathen. He was not a Christian.

Another says, "It is our good breeding that makes the difference between the Anglo-Saxon and the African native." It is not our good breeding. It is something else. It is the consciousness that the Anglo-Saxon mind contains that the other man has not. That consciousness is the consciousness of power, a consciousness of mastery, a consciousness of self-control, and all other varied qualities of the sensitive human mind.

How did they get there? They were established in the mind of the Anglo-Saxon through transmission of those who believed. Consciousness is a growth, an evolution, or an impartation. It is all three in most people.

The incoming of the Spirit of God into the disciples was an impartation of the Spirit of Jesus that brought with it the very conditions of the mind of Christ Himself. He was the one who had throttled death and mastered it and rose up in His own consciousness as King. Therefore, He could say to His disciples,

All power is given unto me in heaven and in earth. Go ye therefore, and teach all nations, baptizing them in the name of the Father, and of the Son, and of the Holy Ghost.
(Matthew 28:18–19)

In other words, [teach the precept of] submitting your body, your soul, and your spirit in an act of union with the Father and the Son and the Holy Ghost, with the purpose of establishing in the individual the conscious knowledge of the living Father and the living Son and the living Spirit. Glory be to God!

When I was a little tyke, I was sprinkled like the rest, and I suppose I squalled just like the rest did. I was not an angel, so far as I know. But when I became a man, I put away childish things.

When I became a man, God revealed the real purpose of what real baptism was supposed to bring into a man's consciousness. And I saw that the purpose of Jesus was to produce in the souls and bodies and spirits of man such a consciousness of the living, triune God that man became a king, a living king. I saw the dignity, I saw the power, I saw the manifestation of Spirit that Jesus purposed should be evident in the life of the person who has been really baptized into the living God—not just baptized in His name, but actually baptized *into* God—buried in Him, inducted into God, inducted into the nature of God the Father, into the nature of God the Son, and into the nature of God the Holy Ghost.

It is almost a sadness to my soul that men should be astonished and surprised at an ordinary, tangible evidence of the power of God. A woman came into the healing rooms on Thursday afternoon with a tumor larger than a full-grown, unborn child, and her physicians and nurse had been fooled, believing it to be such, until nature's period had passed. Then they decided it must be something else.

She came to the healing rooms, and I interviewed her. She said, "Mr. Lake, I have the opinion of several physicians. They are all different, but each has said, 'It is possible it may be a child,' but now the time has passed, and they do not know what to say."

I put my hand upon her for a moment, and I said, "Madam, it is not a child; it is a tumor." She sat down and wept. Her nurse was with her. Her soul was troubled, and she did not receive healing.

She came back on Thursday afternoon for prayer and went away like the rest. But she returned on Friday with her corsets on. She said, "I came to show you that I am perfectly normal. When I retired last night at ten o'clock, there was no evidence that anything had taken place beyond that I felt comfortable and the choking was gone. But when I awoke this morning, I was my normal size."

I said, "Did it disappear in the form of a fluid?"

She said, "There was not an outward sign of any character."

Beloved, what happened to it? It dematerialized, did it not? There was nothing else. The tumor dissolved. It was evaporated, taken out of the system, and was gone in a single night.

I called a friend on the telephone to tell him about it. Another friend was present in the room, and while he still held the receiver in his hand, he turned to his friend and told him about it. The friend said, "My good God, man, that would be a miracle!"

What is a miracle? It is the tangible evidence of the supreme control of the Spirit of God over every character and form of materiality. The tumor disappeared. It was gone. Why? Because the living Spirit of God entered it, and, by the power and working of God, the woman returned to her normal condition. Blessed be His name.

If these evidences of God's presence and power had no value except the mere fact of physical healing, they would not appeal to many thinking minds. Beloved, the power of such an event and of such an act and of such a sign is in this: it shows us that all things are possible through living, positive, actual contact with the Spirit of God. Blessed be His name.

I talked with the husband of the lady—one of the most profane men I have ever known—until Friday morning. He said to me, "Mr. Lake, when I got up on Friday morning and saw my wife, I said, 'I will never again take that name upon my lips in vain.'" And he has walked softly, and a new light is shining in his soul, and a new presence has made itself evident to that man.

Salvation is the best thing that the mind of God ever evolved. Salvation, real salvation, bless God, is that blessed working of God by the Spirit that has for its one objective the absolute transformation of a man—body and soul and spirit—into the likeness of Jesus Christ. And there is no man on earth that could imagine Jesus Christ going around with a big tumor stuck on Him anywhere. Why? Bless God, He did not have any tumors in His soul or in His spirit, either. Why? Because all His nature was joined in complete and holy union with the living God, and the life and nature and substance of God's being, which is the Holy Ghost, flowed through the spirit and soul and body of Jesus alike.

What marvelous union was accomplished through the consent of His own will, without which Jesus Christ Himself could never have been the spotless Lamb of God! But by saying "Yes" to God, by yielding His nature with His "Yes," He permitted the mighty Spirit of God to possess His life and accomplish the will of God in Him and through Him. Blessed be His precious name!

Men are afraid to say yes to God. When a young man, I sat in a little meeting one night when the Spirit was talking to my heart. I said, "If I am going to be a Christian, I cannot do this, and I cannot do that." Oh, mighty God, it almost makes my soul vomit in these days to think of the average conception a man has of Christianity.

About 90 percent of so-called Christianity is all spelled with four letters: D-O-N'-T. Don't do this and don't do that—the individual restraining himself, putting himself in a harness, walking according to laws and ordinances, etc. Why, bless God, Christianity is all contained in two letters: B-E. Not performing acts, but *being* the thing that God purposed.

I was in a meeting in Los Angeles on one occasion. An old black minister[6] was conducting the services, and he had the funniest vocabulary that any man ever had. But I want to tell you, there were doctors and lawyers and professors listening to marvelous things coming from that man's lips. It was not what he said in words, but it was what he said from his spirit to my heart that showed me he had more of God in his life than any man I had ever met up to that time. It was the God in him that was attracting people.

There was one man who insisted on getting up and talking every little while. Some people have a mania for talking. Every once in a while, he would get up and interrupt, and the old minister had endured it for a long time. Presently, he got up again, and the old man stuck his finger out and said, "In the name of Jesus Christ, sit down." He did not sit down. He fell down, and his friends carried him out.

That is only one manifestation of the living fact of what Christianity is: the divine power of Jesus Christ, by the Holy Ghost, filling a man's soul and body, bless God, flashing through his nature like a holy flame, accomplishing the will of God.

The idea that man may be the temple of the Holy Ghost brings a demand on his consciousness that nothing else in the world can bring. If God has ordained that my spirit and my soul and my body, and

---

[6] Note: Lake is referring to William J. Seymour and the Azusa Street Revival.

yours, may become the living, conscious temple of His Spirit—that He, God, will live in us and manifest Himself through us by His Spirit—what kind of demand does it bring upon us?

We can understand then what was in the mind of the apostle when he said, *"What manner of persons ought ye to be in all holy conversation and godliness?"* (2 Peter 3:11).

Why is it that people are slow to yield themselves to the control and government and guidance of the Spirit of God? Why is it that there is not a divine passion in our hearts that such a blessed control should be made a possibility? Shall you and I today assert our own little humanity and walk according to our own light, or shall we, as wise men, as those who seek the most divine in life, say yes to God and let God take our being, inhabit our being, and let Him live His life in us, and then He will manifest His life through us?

I have a brother, a splendid fellow, a finely educated man, a professor. I returned from Africa some years ago, and we were visiting together. As we sat visiting, my sister, who was present, said, "John, I have some old neighbors over here. They are old German people, and they are having a very hard time. The old man died, and one of the sisters died. This thing happened and that thing happened, and finally the son, who was a shipbuilder, fell one day and was carried to the hospital, and they say his leg has to be amputated. Gangrene has set in. The physicians have amputated the toe and a piece of the foot, and now they say the leg has to be amputated. The old mother has been sitting in a wheelchair, a rheumatic cripple, for two and a half years and cannot move."

My brother and I had been having somewhat of a discussion over this thing. He said, "Jack, don't you think these things are all psychological?"

I said, "Not much."

He said, "I think it is."

He said, "Don't you think it is a demonstration of the power of mind over matter?"

And I said, "No. If that was all it is, you could give just as good a demonstration as I could."

After a while, my sister said, "I have been across the street and made arrangements for you to come and pray for these people."

I said, "All right, Jim, come along."

I said to the old lady, "Mother, how long have you been here?"

And she replied, "I have been here two and a half years." She said, "It is awful hard. Not just hard to sit here all the time, but I suffer night and day, with no moment of relaxation from acute suffering in these two and a half years."

As I listened to her, the flame of God came into my soul, and I said, "You rheumatic devil, in the name of Jesus Christ, I will blot you out if it is the last thing

I ever do in the world." And, laying my hands on her, I looked to heaven and called on God to cast that devil out and set her free. I said to her, "Mother, in the name of Jesus Christ, get up and walk." And she arose and walked.

We went into the other room where the son was, whose leg was to be amputated. I sat for a few minutes and told him of the power of God. I said, "We have come to you with a message of Jesus Christ, and we have not just come with the message, but with the power of God." Again, laying my hands on the limb, I said, "In the name of the living God, they shall never amputate this limb," and it was healed.

I was gone for three to six months and then stopped at my sister's home once again. The young lady called and said, "You must come across and see my mother and brother. They are so well." I called and found the old lady very happy. She said, "Oh, Jake, he is not at home. Why, he is so well, he went down to the saloon and danced all night!"

I waited to see Jake, and I tried to tell him something about the living God that he had felt in his body, and who wanted to take possession of his soul and reveal the nature of Jesus Christ in him.

Five years passed by, and I returned again to the United States and was stopping at my sister's home. She said, "Do you remember some people that you prayed for across the road? Here is Jake now, coming from his work." We sat on the porch and talked, and I said, "Well, Jake, how is it?"

"Oh," he said, "I do not understand it all, but something has been going on and going on. It is in me. First, I could not go to the dance, and next I could not drink beer, and next my tobacco did not taste good, and then a joy came into my heart, and then I found it was just Jesus."

Born of God—the nature of man brought into union with God by the Holy Ghost. Blessed be His precious name.

This congregation has perhaps been blessed with the continued manifestation of the presence of God beyond that of any other congregation in the world. This city has been blessed with the manifestation of God's presence perhaps beyond that of any other city in the world. Yet, the eyes of many are closed. They have not seen God. Some have seen Brother Lake, some have seen Brother Westwood, but not all have seen God, the living God. Many need the continued process of the Spirit of God in their souls that went on in the heart of Jake, revealing the nature of Christ until all his being said yes to God, and he became a Christian in deed and in truth. Blessed be God.

I leave you today with this message of God: Open your soul to Him, and let the blessed living Spirit of

God have entrance into your nature. Say yes to God. Say yes to God.

John the Baptist was a prophet. One day, as Jesus stood among His friends, John said, *"Behold the Lamb of God, which taketh away the sin of the world"* (John 1:29), and *"I indeed baptize you with water unto repentance: but...he shall baptize you with the Holy Ghost, and with fire"* (Matthew 3:11).

There is a baptism that belongs to Jesus. It is in His supreme right and control. No other angel or man can bestow it. It comes from Him alone. *"He which baptizeth with the Holy Ghost"* (John 1:33). So the individual who wants the Holy Ghost must come into definite, conscious contact with Jesus Christ Himself. Bless God.

Chapter Twenty-three

Discernment

Sermon

1 Corinthians 12:8–12

My first great interest in Africa was stimulated when I was a child, through reading of Livingstone's travels and explorations and of Stanley finding Livingstone in the heart of Africa and still more by reading of Stanley's trip across the continent and down the Congo.[7]

As the years of my boyhood passed, I became conscious of a certain operation of my spirit, which I shall endeavor to describe.

In my sleep, and sometimes during my waking hours, it seemed to me as if I was present in Africa instead of America. At such times, I would note the geography of the country, the peculiarities of the landscape, and the characteristics of the various tribes of native people. I became deeply sympathetic with the efforts of the Boers as I watched them endeavoring to establish their republics.

---

[7] In 1866, explorer David Livingstone went to Africa to search for the source of the Nile River, then he disappeared. Five years later, reporter Henry Morton Stanley set out to find him, and on November 10, 1871, he did. Source: "The Scoop of the Century: Was getting the story worth the cost?" *National Geographic World Magazine* (available online at www.nationalgeographic.com).

As I reached manhood, these excursions in the spirit became more intelligent to me. On one occasion while in the attitude of prayer, I approached South Africa from the Indian Ocean and traveled through Zululand over into the mountains of Basutoland. I noted the distinctions of the tribal characteristics as I passed through these states. I also traveled through the Orange Free State and the Transvaal from Basutoland to Johannesburg.

This excursion, projection of spirit-consciousness, or whatever it may be termed, occurred during hours of communion with God in prayer.

While meditating and praying while on the sea on my way to Africa, I would become suddenly conscious of the political conditions of South Africa. I would feel the struggles of the various political elements in their contest for supremacy. Then again, I would realize the condition of the country financially and still again see the religious aspects of the nation. I saw the predominating thought that bound the Boer people as a nation to the Dutch church and the struggles of the civilized native people to attain a religious independence.

While in the spirit, I comprehended not only present fact, but my consciousness would project itself into the future so that I saw the train of national events that were yet to take place. And I also saw the West Coast of Africa, when they had become great commercial seaports with lines of railways extending up into the Transvaal.

Much of this vision I have seen fulfilled at this writing, namely, the uniting of the South African states into a national union (Natal, Orange Free State, Cape Colony, and the Transvaal); the great religious upheaval; the settlement of political and financial problems, etc. I saw the conquest of German Southwest Africa by the British, including some of the battle scenes of the present war there.

No one could realize, unless he had been associated with me in the work in Africa, how thorough this knowledge of the conditions in Africa was made to me. This was not the result of reading, for I had read practically nothing of Africa since my childhood.

In traveling through the country after my arrival, there was nothing new. I had seen it all in advance and could recollect times and circumstances when, in my visions of Africa, I had visited one city or another.

This knowledge of affairs was of inestimable value to me when I was actually on the ground. Businessmen and statesmen alike frequently expressed surprise at the intimate knowledge I possessed of conditions in the land, little realizing how this knowledge had come to me.

This spiritual consciousness of conditions, or great gift of knowledge, continued with me throughout my first years as president of the Apostolic Church of South Africa.

It was my custom to dictate my letters in the morning before going to my office or out among the sick for the duties of the day. At such times, if I wanted to write a letter, for instance, to Cape Town, Pietermaritzburg, Pretoria, or some other place, I would bow my head in quiet before God for a few moments. While in this attitude, there would be born in my consciousness the conditions of the assembly or district or town, as the case might be. I could see the difficulties the brethren were having there, if any, and hundreds of times have written, revealing to them an inside knowledge of the conditions among them that they were sure no one knew about.

In the conduct of our native work, this feature was so marked that, after a time, an adage grew up among the natives: "You cannot fool Brother Lake; God shows him." Many, many times when the natives would come and present perhaps only one side of the matter, I would be able to tell them the whole truth concerning the difficulty.

One time, a man came from Robertson and made charges against a brother who was one of the elders in the work there. When he got through, I said to him, "Brother, let us bow our heads in prayer." Instantly, I seemed to be in Robertson. I observed the assembly, saw the various brethren there, and noted their piety and devotion to God, and I saw that the condition was almost the reverse as it had been presented. The man himself was the troublemaker.

On another occasion, a woman came to me several times requesting prayer for her deliverance from drunkenness. I urged upon her the necessity of re-pentance unto God, confession of her sins, etc. She assured me many times that she had done all of this.

One day, she came while I was resting on the cot. My wife brought her into the room. She knelt, weeping, by the cot. As usual, she asked me to pray for deliverance. I said to her, "What about the two hundred and fifty pounds' sterling worth of jewelry that you stole from such and such a home?" She threw up her hands with an exclamation of despair, supposing that I would deliver her to the police or tell the party from whom she had stolen it. I calmed her by assurance that, since I was a minister of Christ, no one would know from me concerning the matter. I regarded the knowledge as sacred before God, because God had revealed it to me in order to assist her out of her difficulty. She was delivered from her drunkenness and remained a sober woman, working earnestly in the vineyard of the Lord.

Some days afterward, a woman came to me, saying, "I have heard that So-and-so (naming the lady of whom I have spoken) has been converted, and I know she must have confessed to you that she stole jewelry from my home." I explained to her that, even if such a confession had been made, as a minister of Jesus Christ, I could not reveal it and would not reveal it.

As we conversed, I told her I believed God had sent her in order that we might discuss together the forgiveness of God. I showed her that God expected us to forgive, even as we are forgiven; indeed, that we are commanded to forgive. (See Matthew 6:14–15.) The Spirit gave me such a consciousness of the forgiveness of God that, as I presented it to her, it seemed to flow in liquid love from my soul. She broke down and wept, asking me to pray for her that God would deliver her from her own sins and establish in her the knowledge and consciousness of His presence and life. She left saying, "Tell So-and-so that as far as the jewelry is concerned, I shall never mention it again. There will be no prosecution, and by the grace of God, I forgive her."

My wife possessed the spirit of discernment in a more marked degree than I did, especially concerning difficulties in people's lives, particularly regarding those seeking healing. She had the power to reveal the reason they were not blessed of God.

It was my custom in receiving the sick in my office to let them stand in a line, and I would pray for them, laying hands on all as they passed me. Some would not receive healing, and their suffering would continue. Some would receive healing in part, and some were instantly healed. I would pass those who received no healing into the adjoining room, and when I had finished praying for the multitude, I would bring my wife into the room where these unhealed ones were. She would go close to one and would say, in substance, "Your difficulty is that, at such and such a time, you committed such and such a sin, which has not been repented of and confessed." To another, perhaps it would be, "God wants you to make restitution for such and such an act that you committed at such and such a time." To another, "The pride of your heart and the love of the world have not been laid on the altar of Christ."

Upon hearing the inner things of their hearts revealed, many would bow at once and confess their sins to God. We would pray for them again, and the Lord would heal them. Some would go away unrepentant. Some would go through the motions of repentance, but it was not of the heart, and they would not be healed. Thus we are taught to value highly the gift of God, of which Paul speaks in 1 Corinthians 12:10, "*to another the discerning of spirits.*"

The Spirit of God is like the bread that the disciples held in their hands. When they broke it and distributed it to the multitudes, there was more remaining than when they began. (See John 6:11–13.) The Spirit of God is *creative, generative,* and *constructive,* and the more you give, the more you receive. Jesus laid down a perpetual law when He said,

Give, and it shall be given unto you; good measure, pressed down, and shaken together, and running over, shall men give into your bosom. For with the same measure that ye mete withal it shall be measured to you again. (Luke 6:38)

Chapter Twenty-four

Holiness unto the Lord

Sermon

Spokane, Washington • March 6, 1916

Holiness is the character of God. The very substance of His being and essence of His nature is purity. The purpose of God in the salvation of mankind is to produce in man a kindred holiness, a radiant purity like that of God Himself. If God were unable to produce such purity in man, then His purpose in man would be a failure, and the object of the sacrifice of Jesus Christ would be a miscarriage instead of a triumph.

The triumph of Jesus Christ was attained through His willingness to be led by the Spirit of God. The triumph of the Christian can be attained only in a similar manner. Even though God has baptized a soul with the Holy Spirit, there yet remains for the person, as with Jesus, the present necessity of walking in humility and permitting the Spirit of God to be his absolute guide.

The unveiling of consciousness, of the desire of the flesh, of the sensuality of the nature and the thoughts of man and the revelation of adverse tendencies—all are part of God's purpose and are necessary for growth in God. How can the nature of man be changed except that nature is first revealed? So there arises in the heart the desire and prayer for the Spirit of God to eject, crucify, and destroy every tendency of opposition to the Holy Spirit.

Think not that you shall attain the highest in God until within your own soul a heavenly longing to be like Him who gave His life for us possesses your heart. Think not to come within the court of God with stains upon your garments. Think not that heaven can smile upon a nature fouled through evil contact. Think not that Christ can dwell in temples seared by flames of hate. No! The heart of man must first be purged by holy fire and washed from every stain by cleansing blood. Don't you know that the person whose nature is akin to God's must ever feel the purging power of Christ within?

He who would understand the ways of God must trust the Spirit's power to guide and keep. He who would tread the paths where angels tread must realize seraphic purity himself. Such is the nature of God, such the working of the Spirit's power, such the attainment of the person who overcomes. In him the joy and power of God shall be. Through him the healing streams of life shall flow. To him heaven's gates are opened wide. In him the kingdom is revealed.

Interpretation of a Message in Tongues

Fear not to place thy hand within the nail-pierced palm. Fear not to trust His guidance. The way He trod is marked by bleeding feet and wet with many tears. He leadeth thee aright, and heaven's splendor soon shall open to thy spirit, and thou shalt know that all triumphant souls—those who have overcome indeed—have found their entrance by this path into the realms of light.

Chapter Twenty-five

The Holy Ghost Made Manifest

Sermon

Findlay, Ohio • April 26, 1914

That blessed, old, simple story is burning in my spirit. Let's read John 1:6–13.

There was a man sent from God, whose name was John. The same came for a witness, to bear witness of the Light, that all men through him might believe. He was not that Light, but was sent to bear witness of that Light. That was the true Light, which lighteth every man that cometh into the world. He was in the world, and the world was made by him, and the world knew him not. He came unto his own, and his own received him not. But as many as received him, to them gave he power to become the sons of God, even to them that believe on his name: which were born, not of blood, nor of the will of the flesh, nor of the will of man, but of God.

I feel somehow this morning that, as we are a representative body of men and women whose business it is in life to proclaim and exemplify the gospel of Jesus

Christ, the presentation of the Son of God as the Savior of the world is the greatest thing we have before us.

God is looking upon us and expecting us to give that satisfactory demonstration of the Christ-life to other men so that the world may desire Jesus as the Son of God, and that men may look forward to and long for the day when the Christ shall come and when He will establish the kingdom of Jesus Christ in the earth. Anything else than this does not seem to me to be worthy of those who have had the special privilege of living in these times when the Spirit is being poured out upon all flesh.

Interpretation of a Message in Tongues

The days of our childhood in the things of God have gone by, and the days of maturity in knowledge of God have now dawned upon us.

God is demanding from us a demonstration of the power of God, the love of God, and the character of Christ that is worthy of the day, the hour, the message, and the time in which we live. Now is a special time when the Spirit of God is being poured upon mankind in preparation for the hour when Jesus shall return and call the saints of God to His own glory. May we receive from Him during this period of exceptional privilege the instruction, development, capacity, and empowerment that those who are to come again with Him into the establishment of His kingdom receive. May we take part and place with our Lord Jesus Christ in the government of this old world in love, righteousness, purity, holiness, truth, and verity throughout the kingdom age.

Our God, this morning, calls your heart and mine from an ordinary understanding and consciousness of the gospel of Jesus Christ to a Holy Ghost-quickening consciousness, to that especially illuminated, blessedly glorified, spiritual understanding of the Word of God and the mind of God. This is in order that we may be peculiar men and peculiar women, living a peculiar life—peculiar in love, peculiar in holiness, peculiar in reverence for the living God, peculiar in knowing the secrets of divine power and government.

And to Thee, O God our Father, we lift our hearts and ask that Thou will help us, that we may be worthy of the high calling that God our Father hath bestowed upon us, through the mercy and sacrifice of Jesus Christ. That we may live, O God our Father, according to Thy mind and according to Thy heart, according to Thy way and according to Thy will, in God.

Shall it be that the voices of all men, and especially the voices of those who realize conscious salvation through the precious blood of Jesus Christ, ring forth in this world God's new message? Shall our voices be raised in the peculiar Spirit and power of God, manifesting Christ in man in these days, giving the message of God, the Savior of mankind, as the Redeemer and Sanctifier of man, as He who joys and dwells in the holiness of His children?

God cannot look with any degree of toleration upon sin and selfishness, but looks with the eye of pity, sacrifice, and holiness upon man, discovering in the very depths of our nature that which is unlike His living, precious holiness. And He desires that our nature shall be changed, our hearts shall be lifted up to Him in the joy and praise and gladness of those who know and understand and realize the sanctity of being permitted to be children of God, washed in His precious blood, crowned with His Spirit, looking for His glory.

So, this morning, our blessed Lord asks all of us who are discouraged, who are weary, who have lived in the ordinary routine of life, that our hearts shall be lifted up to Him, and that we shall realize that He desires in a peculiar way to stamp it upon our hearts that the Son of God, Jesus Christ, our Savior and Redeemer, died on the cross and His body lay in the grave. Yet, the power of God was sufficient to come and raise Him up into life and quicken Him, strengthen Him, and lift Him up into the place of triumph. Yes, He ascended into the heavenlies and sat down in triumph at the right hand of God.

Therefore, let our hearts faint not, but with a new hope and a new determination yield ourselves to God that we, too, may be lifted up indeed, out of the insecurity of the present hour and moment into the life triumphant and heavenly and holy, for our dwelling place is not on earth, but our dwelling is in the heavens.

The peculiar work of the Holy Spirit in this present hour is according to our present need. Yes, even that our consciousness may be so quickened and our understanding of God and His ways so enlightened, that our hearts may take on a new hope and our lives ascend into heavenly places in Christ Jesus, where all things are beneath our feet and where the powers of earth and the things of life no longer drag us down, but where in the power of the Holy Spirit we move and walk as triumphant men and triumphant women, conquerors of disease, sin, death, and the powers of darkness that drag us down day by day.

The Lord wants us to pray.

The Spirit of the Lord, as we prayed, told my soul that the peculiar sin of the present hour among the children of God is a peculiar spiritual lethargy that has been permitted to gradually steal over our souls, robbing us of the quickened consciousness and understanding of the blessed Holy Ghost and of His presence; that instead of lifting up our hearts and welcoming Him, we have descended into a study of the understanding of His ways and works and methods until a dimness has come over our spirits.

God wants once again to take us out of the natural things, the exercise of our natural minds and our natural spirits, into the Holy Ghost, into the ascended life, into the life in heavenly places in Christ Jesus, where the Spirit of God in enduement and power rests upon our souls. And returning, filled with His presence and glory, we may bring into this world the quickened consciousness of the Lord Jesus Christ:

- That the transforming power of the Spirit may be so freely realized that mankind may see and know it is the day of His preparation.

- That our whole lives and beings may be so yielded up to the living God that every heart shall be a vessel through which the Spirit of God shall flow to the blessing of the lost world.

- That the spirit of criticism of one another, and of all men, shall cease within the Christian heart and the enlightened conscience.

- That everyone shall realize that he or she has the possession of the degree and measure of the Holy Ghost that God, in His love, has been able to bestow upon the individual in his or her present state of development.

- That, instead of placing ourselves above another and looking with scorn even upon the sinner, we shall see even as Jesus sees men and understand others even as the heart of Christ understands.

- That in love and mercy and sympathy and compassion, we shall reach out our arms and embrace our fellows and lead them to the Lamb of God that takes away the sin of the world.

When the Christian consciousness and the Christian understanding are illuminated by the presence of the loving God in the measure that God does desire to give us, the world shall give forth an exaltation of the Lord Jesus Christ so pure and holy and true and blessed that all men shall see and know that there is a living God. And the real Christ and living Savior will manifest through the church, the body of Jesus in the world, through whom the manifestation of the living Christ is being given to all men to the glory of God.

So, our blessed God, we lift our hearts up this morning and ask Thee, our blessed God, that You will take out of our spirits every wretched little bit of hidden selfishness that is hidden within us. O God, apply the precious blood of Jesus Christ, that we may be so purified and so illuminated by the Holy Ghost and the glory of God, that we shall give forth that real reflection of the Lord Jesus Christ in the Holy Ghost, for Jesus' sake. Lord God, we ask Thee this morning, as we lift our hands to heaven and as we submit our souls to Thee, as we confess our littleness and our meanness and our self-righteousness, that the blessed Christ shall establish within us the Holy Spirit, who Himself shall manifest the truth of the Spirit, for Jesus' sake.

And our God, we pray Thee that Thou wilt lift up each one into the presence of God, and that Thou wilt put upon us such a consciousness of God, of His love, of His purity, of His holiness, of His power, that, O God, our Christ, our praise to Thee and our worship of God shall be in the beauty of holiness. O God, that we shall worship Thee in spirit and in truth, for Jesus' sake. O we ask, our God, that every hidden thing, everything that would not bear the glory-light of God, shall be driven from our natures. That, O God, our Christ, once again we can stand before Jesus, even as did Nathaniel, an Israelite indeed, in whom was no guile. O God, we ask Thee then that You will sweep from our souls and wash from our natures and cleanse from our hearts every unholy thing, every deceitful thing, Lord Jesus, this devilish spiritual pride that is so subtle. O God, sweep them away. Let us stand, O God our Christ, guileless before our God, for Jesus' sake.

Blessed be Thy name, O God. We worship Thee and lift our hands and our hearts to heaven, and we say this morning, blessed be Thy name. Holy, holy, holy is the Lord. Blessed be His name! Our God, to Thee this morning we offer our praise and worship and adoration and glory and praise and honor unto Thy name forever and ever and ever. Blessed be Thy name. Amen.

Our God, we pray this morning that the blessing and power of God shall so rest upon us, that a yieldedness to the living God and to all the works of the Holy Spirit within us shall be so manifest, our God, that those will be able to lift us up, so that we will be permitted to enter into the exaltation of the Lord Jesus Christ, who has become the Ruler of this universe, King of kings and Lord of lords, with angels and archangels, rejoicing before God because of the triumph of the Son of God, through the spilling of His precious blood for all men and all mankind's acceptance of Him, for Jesus' sake. Amen.

Chapter Twenty-six

Ministry of the Spirit

Sermon

November 24, 1916

One of the most difficult things to bring into the spirit of people is that the Spirit of God is a tangible substance, that it is the essence of God's own being.

We are composed of an earthly materiality; our bodies are largely a composition of water and earth. This may sound a little crude, but the actual composition of a human being is about sixteen buckets of water and one bucketful of earth. I am glad that there is one bucketful of good mud in us. Water, you know, is a composition of gases, so you can see how much gas there is in mankind. But we are not all gas.

Now, the composition of the personality of God— for God has a personality and a being and a substance (spirit is a substance)—that is the thing I am trying to emphasize. All heavenly things are of spiritual substance. The body of the angels is of some substance— not the same character of materiality as our own, for ours is an earthly materiality—but the composition of heavenly things is of a heavenly materiality. In other words, heavenly materiality is spirit. The Word says,

"*God is a Spirit.*" He is a spirit; therefore, "*They that worship him must worship him in spirit*" (John 4:24).

You see, the spirit of man must contact and know the real Spirit of God—know God. We do not know God with our flesh, with our hands, or with our brains. We know God with our spirits. The knowledge of God that our spirits attain may be conveyed and is conveyed to us through the medium of our minds, through the medium of our brains. The effect of God in our bodies comes through the medium of the spirit of man, through the mind of man, into the body of man.

There is a quickening by the Spirit of God so that a man's body, a man's soul or mind, and a man's spirit all alike become blessed, pervaded, and filled with the presence of God Himself in us. The Word of God is wonderfully clear along these lines. For instance, the Word of God says, "*Thou wilt keep him in perfect peace, whose **mind** is stayed on thee*" (Isaiah 26:3). Why? "*Because he trusteth in thee.*" That is the rest that a Christian knows whose mind rests in God in real perfect trust. "*Thou wilt keep him in perfect peace, whose mind is stayed on thee.*"

The Word of God again says that our *flesh* shall rejoice—not our minds—but our very flesh shall rejoice.[8] The presence of God is to be a living presence, not only in the spirit of man, not in the mind of man

---

[8] Note: Lake was possibly referring to Psalm 16:9 or Acts 2:26.

alone, but also in the flesh of man, so that God is known in *all* the departments of our life. We know God in our very flesh; we know God in our minds; we know God in our spirits. Bless His precious name.

The medium by which God undertakes to bless the world is through the transmission of Himself. Now, the Spirit of God is His own substance, the substance of His being, the very nature and quality of the very presence and being and nature of God. Consequently, when we speak of the Spirit of God being transmitted to man and into man, we are not talking about an influence, either spiritual or mental. We are talking about the transmission of the living substance and being of God into your being and into mine—not a mental effect, but a living substance—the living being and actual life transmitted, imparted, coming from God into your being, into my being. Bless God!

That is the secret of the abundant life of which Jesus spoke. Jesus said, *"I am come that they might have life, and that they might have it **more abundantly**"* (John 10:10). The reason we have the more abundant life is that, upon receiving God into our being, all the springs of our being are quickened by His living presence. Consequently, if we are living today and we receive God, we live life in a fuller measure. We live life with a greater energy because we become the recipients of the energy of the living God in addition to our normal energy, through the reception of His being, His nature, His life into ours.

The wonderful measure by which the human being is capable of receiving God is demonstrated by some of the incidents in the Word of God. For instance, the most remarkable in the Scriptures is the transfiguration of Jesus Himself, where—with Peter, James, and John—the Spirit of God came upon Him so powerfully that it radiated out through His being until His clothes glistened as white as the light and His face shone as bright as the sun. (See Matthew 17:2.)

Now, one must be the recipient of the light, glory, and power of God before he or she can manifest it. Jesus demonstrated these two facts: (1) the marvelous capacity of the nature of man to receive God into his being, and (2) the marvelous capacity of the nature of man to reveal God. In the glory that glistened even from His apparel, in the glory of God that made His face radiant and glowing, He demonstrated man's capacity to reveal God.

The human being is God's marvelous, wonderful instrument, the most marvelous and wonderful of all the creation of God in its capacity to receive and reveal God. Paul received so much of God into his being that when men brought handkerchiefs and he took them in his hands, and the women brought their aprons and handed them to him, the handkerchiefs and aprons became so impregnated with that living Spirit of God (that living substance of God's being) that when they were carried to one who was sick or possessed of devils—the Word says when they laid the handkerchiefs or aprons on them—the Spirit of the living God passed from the handkerchiefs or aprons into the sick man or into the insane man; and the sick were healed, and the devils were cast out. (See Acts 19:11–12.)

You see, people have been so in the habit of putting Jesus in a class by Himself that they have failed to recognize that He has made provision for the same living Spirit of God that dwelt in His own life, and of which He Himself was a living manifestation, to inhabit your being and mine, just as the Spirit inhabited the being of Jesus or Paul.

There is no more marvelous manifestation in the life of Jesus than that manifestation of healing through the apostle Paul.

Do you remember the incident of the woman who touched the hem of Jesus' garment? Knowing how His whole being, His whole nature, radiated that wondrous, blessed life of God of which He was Himself the living manifestation, she said within herself, "If I can but touch His garment, I shall be healed." (See Matthew 9:21; Mark 5:28.) So she succeeded after much effort in touching the hem of His garment, and as she touched the hem of His garment, there flowed into her body the quickening lifestream, and she felt in her body that she was made whole of the plague. And Jesus, being conscious that something had flowed from Him, said to Peter, "Who touched Me?"

Peter replied, "Why, Master, You see the crowd, and do You still ask, 'Who touched Me?'"

"I know *somebody* touched Me," He said, "for I perceive that *virtue* has gone out of Me." (See Mark 5:25–34.) If you will analyze that Greek word, you will see it means the life or substance of His being, the quickening, living power of God, the very nature and being of God.

If I transmit to another the virtue of my life, I simply transmit a portion of my life to another—the life power that is in me, blessed be God. The life of God that flows through me is transmitted to another, and so it was with Jesus.

Now then, it is a fact that people brought to Paul handkerchiefs and aprons, which became impregnated with the Spirit of God, and people were healed when they touched them. This is a demonstration in itself that a material substance can become impregnated with the same living Spirit of God.

In my church in South Africa, we published a paper in ten thousand lots. We would have the publishers send them to the tabernacle, and we would lay them out in packages of one or two hundred all around the front of the platform. At the evening service, I would call certain ones of the congregation that I knew to be in contact with the living God to come and kneel around and lay their hands on those packages of papers. We asked God not only that the reading matter in the paper might be a blessing to the individual and that the message of Christ come through the words printed on the paper, but we also asked God to make the very substance of the paper itself become filled with the Spirit of God, just like the handkerchiefs became filled with the Spirit of God.

If I were in my tabernacle now, I could show you thousands of letters in my files from all quarters of the world, from people telling me that when they received our paper, the Spirit came upon them, and they were healed, or when they received the paper, the joy of God came into their hearts, or they received the paper and were saved unto God.

One woman wrote from South America, who said, "I received your paper. When I received it into my hands, my body began to vibrate so I could hardly sit on the chair, and I did not understand it. I laid the paper down, and I took the paper up again after a while. As soon as I had it in my hands, I shook again. I laid the paper down and took it in my hands a third time, and presently, the Spirit of God came upon me so powerfully that I was baptized in the Holy Ghost."

Beloved, don't you see that this message and this quality of the Spirit contains the thing that confuses all the philosophers and all practice of philosophy in the world? It shows the clearest distinction that characterizes the real religion of Jesus Christ and makes it distinct from all other religions and all other ministries.

The ministry of the Christian is the ministry of the Spirit. He not only ministers words to another, but he also ministers the Spirit of God. It is the Spirit of God that inhabits the words, that speaks to the spirit of another and reveals Christ in and through him.

In the old days when I was in Africa, I would walk into the native meetings when I did not understand the languages and listen to the preacher preach for an hour, and I did not understand a word he said. But my soul was blessed by the presence of the Spirit of God.

As bishop of the church, I went from place to place holding conferences here and there among white and native people. In many of them, people would speak either in English or Dutch. But I was just as much blessed when a Dutchman spoke and I did not understand him as when an Englishman spoke. Why? Because the thing that blessed my soul was the living Spirit of God. Perhaps I had heard better words than his, perhaps clearer explanation of the Scriptures than he could give, but I was blessed by the presence of God. The thing that the individual was ministering to my soul was the living Spirit of God.

The ministry of the Christian is the ministry of the Spirit. Other men have intellectuality, but the Christian is supposed to be the possessor of the Spirit. He possesses something that no other man in the whole world possesses—that is, the Spirit of the living God.

LETTERS PRESENTED FOR PRAYER

These letters are to dear people all over the land, and I have this feeling that I would like to revive among us that blessed, old practice of believing God for the very substance of the letter, the paper, or handkerchief to become so filled with the Spirit of the Lord God that, when it comes into their hands, they would not only feel blessed by the words of the letter, but the blessed Spirit of God would flow into their beings out of the substance of the paper itself.

That is Christianity. That is the gospel of Jesus Christ. That is the thing that goes thousands of miles beyond psychological influence. If you want a clear distinction between psychological religions, as they are called, or mental science, you can see it in a minute. The real Christian ministers the real Spirit of God, the substance of His being. There should never be the necessity for misunderstanding along these lines in the minds of anyone.

A minister of Jesus Christ is as far removed above the realm of psychological influences as heaven is above the earth. Blessed be God. He ministers God Himself into the very spirits and souls and bodies of men. That is the reason the Christian throws down the bars of this nature and invites God to come in and take possession of his being. And the incoming of God into our bodies, into our souls, into our spirits accomplishes marvelous things in the nature of man.

A man came into my healing room one day and said, "I am almost ashamed to call myself a man because I have simply indulged the animal part of my nature so that I am more a beast than a man. You say, 'Why don't you quit such a life?' I have not the strength of my being to do so. Unless something takes place that will deliver me from this condition, I do not know what I will do."

I tried to show him what the gospel of Jesus Christ was. I tried to show him that through living in the animal state, thinking animal thoughts, surrounding himself with beastly suggestions, and contacting the spirit of bestiality everywhere, that the animal element had taken such possession that it predominated in his nature. I said, "My son, if the gospel means anything, it means there shall be a transference of nature. Instead of this living hell that is present in your being, the living, holy God should flow into your

185

life and cast out the devil, dispossess the beast, and reign in your members."

We knelt to pray. Today, he came back with tears in his eyes and said, "Mr. Lake, I feel I can shake hands with you now. I am a beast no more. I am a man."

Yesterday, a dear woman was present in our afternoon service. She had a tumor that for ten months the physicians believed to be an unborn child. She came with her nurse a few days ago to the healing rooms and told me her symptoms. The thing that fooled the physicians was that there was a movement that they considered similar to life movement, and the result was that during all these months, they believed the woman would become a mother, until the normal time had long passed. She was the first one to be prayed for after the Thursday afternoon service.

Today, she returned and said, "Mr. Lake, I want you to see me. I have my corsets on; I am perfectly normal. When I went to bed, I was not aware that anything had taken place except that the choking had ceased and I felt comfortable. I was not aware of any diminution in my size. But when I awoke this morning, I was perfectly normal."

I said, "How did the tumor disappear? Was it in the form of a fluid?"

She said, "No, nothing came from my person."

Now, I am going to ask you, where did a great tumor like that go to? What happened to it? (A voice in audience says, "It dematerialized.")

Yes, the living Spirit of God absolutely dematerialized the tumor, and the process was accomplished in one night while the woman slept. That is one of God's methods of surgical operations, isn't it?

Beloved, even her tumor became filled with the Spirit of God. The effect of the Spirit of God in that tumor was so mighty, so powerful, that it was completely dissolved.

That is the secret of the ministry of Jesus Christ. That is the secret of the ministry of Christianity. That is the reason that the real Christian who lives in union with the living God and possesses His Spirit has a ministry that no other man in the world possesses. That is the reason the real Christian here has a revelation of Jesus Christ and His almightiness and His power to save that no other human in all the world possesses. Why? He is full and experiences in his own soul the dissolving power of the Spirit of God that takes sin out of his life and makes him a free man in Christ Jesus. Blessed be His name forever.

A few weeks ago, a dear woman called me over the telephone and said, "I have a young friend who is a drunkard, and the habit has such power over him that he will go to any excess to obtain alcohol. Dry state or no dry state, he has to have it. He is an intelligent fellow. He wants to be free. We have invited him to my home for prayer, and he is here now. I want you to join me in prayer for him."

I said, "All right, but first, call one of your neighbors to join you in prayer for this man; then, when you are ready, call me on the phone, and Brother Westwood and Mrs. Patterson and I will join you in prayer." She called me in a little while, and we united our hearts in prayer for the young man, who was on the other side of the city. About twenty minutes afterward, he arose from his knees and with tears in his eyes, he took the woman by the hand and said, "I am a man of sense. I know when something has taken place with me, and the appetite has disappeared." That is the ministry of the Spirit, the ministry of God to man. Blessed be His name.

Isn't it a marvelous, wonderful thing that God has ordained an arrangement whereby man becomes God's own copartner and coworker in the ministry of the Spirit? "The church, which is His body." (See Colossians 1:24.) Just as Jesus Christ was the human body through which the living Spirit was ministered to mankind, so God has arranged that the living church—not the dead members, but the living church, alive with the Spirit of the living God—should minister that quickening life to others and thereby become a copartner, a laborer together with God. Blessed be His name forever.

Men have mystified and philosophized over the gospel of Jesus, but the gospel is as simple as can be. Just as God lived and operated through the body of the Man, Jesus, so Jesus, the Man on the throne, operates in and through the Christian and also through His body, the church, in the world. Just as Jesus was the representative of God the Father, so the church is the representative of Christ. And as Jesus yielded Himself unto all righteousness, so the church should yield herself to do all the will of God.

The secret of Christianity is in *being*. It is in being a possessor of the nature of Jesus Christ. In other words, it is being Christ in character, Christ in demonstration, Christ in agency of transmission. When a person gives himself to the Lord and becomes a child of God, a Christian, he is a Christ-man. All that he does and all that he says from that time forth should be the will and the words and the doings of Jesus, just as absolutely and entirely as He spoke and did the will of the Father.

Chapter Twenty-seven

The Power of the Spirit

Sermon

The life of a Christian without the indwelling power of the Spirit in the heart is weariness to the flesh. It is an obedience to commandments and an endeavor to walk according to a pattern that you have no power [of your own] to follow. But bless God, the Christian life that is lived by the impulse of the Spirit of Christ within your soul becomes a joy and a power and a glory. Blessed be God.

The power in the Spirit of Christ only becomes applicable in our life according to the vision and the application of our thought to our own need. The air is filled with electricity. It is in the skies; it is under the water. There is nowhere you can go to escape from it. Consequently, it is usable everywhere, *if* you take possession of it. So it is with the Spirit of Christ. The mode or means or manner by which the soul of man takes possession of the power of God is through the attitude of the soul and mind of man toward it.

I may live all the days of my life in a quiescent, dreamy state, never becoming conscious of the power of God in my life. On the other hand, I can lend my soul and mind to God in active force until the

Spirit of the living God so impregnates my life and flashes from my being that, like the Lord Jesus, the evidences and manifestations of that divine life is given to other men.

THE GIFT OF TONGUES IN OPERATION

One evening in my own tabernacle, a young girl by the name of Hilda Daniels, about sixteen or eighteen, suddenly became overpowered by the Spirit of God. She arose and stood on the platform beside me. I recognized at once that the Lord had given her the message. So I simply stopped preaching and waited while the Spirit of God came upon her. She began to chant in some language I did not know and make gestures like a Mohammedan priest would make when chanting prayers.

Away down in the back of the house, I observed a young East Indian, whom I knew. He became enraptured and commenced to walk gradually up the aisle. No one disturbed him, and he proceeded up the aisle until he got to the front and stood looking into the girl's face with intense amazement.

When her message had ceased, I said to him, "What is it?"

He said, "Oh, she speaks my language."

I said, "What does she say?" And he came up on the platform and stood beside me and gave a gist of her message.

"She tells me that salvation comes from God; that in order to save men, Jesus Christ, who was God, became man; that one man cannot save another; that Mohammed was a man like other men and had no power to save a man from his sins. But Jesus was God, and He had power to impart His Spirit to me and make me like God."

One day, I stood at the railway station in Logansport, Indiana, waiting for my train. I observed a group of Italian men, apparently laborers, sitting on a bench. They were going out somewhere to work. As I walked up and down the platform, I said, "Oh God, how much I would like to be able to talk to these men about the living Christ and His power to save."

The Spirit said, "You can."

I stepped over to them, and as I approached them, I observed myself commencing to speak in some foreign language. I addressed one of the group, and he instantly answered me in Italian. I asked where he was from, and he replied, "Naples." For fifteen minutes, God let me tell of the truth of Christ and the power of God to that group of Italian laborers, in Italian, a language I had no knowledge of.

Again and again at intervals, God has permitted such things to occur in my life. But, beloved, that is not the real "gift of tongues" yet. It is a little flash, a gleam, but one day there will come from heaven God's blessed shower that will so anoint the souls of men that they will speak in every language man speaks in, by the power of God. The message of the Christ will be given through these anointed hearts to the nations of the world. Said Jesus, "This gospel of the kingdom must first be preached to all nations," etc. (See Matthew 24:14.)

May I refer you once more to history? The Moravian missionaries went to Japan about a hundred years ago. Other missionaries spend long periods trying to acquire the language, but these missionaries, history records, went into a prayer meeting for six weeks, night and day, and came out of that meeting speaking the Japanese languages fluently.

SORROW OVER SOULS BLINDED TO THE FULL GOSPEL

These things only demonstrate to you and me the necessity of keeping the soul open to the ever-growing consciousness of God. Is healing a wonder? No, the marvel is that men have remained blind to the power of God for so long. How is it that you and I, raised in Christian homes, reading the Word of God, praying to our Father God, failed to comprehend that the power of God through Christ is able to save a man from all his sins and all his sicknesses?

Our souls have caught just a little flash, a little larger revelation of the living God through the blessed Word and through the Holy Spirit, the divine power to make it real. But, my brother, beyond the soul is the great ocean of God. We are just paddling around the edge yet.

When I was ready to leave Pullman last week, my friends gathered around. Many of them said, "Brother, we never heard anything like it. What a marvelous meeting. What numbers of wonderful healings!" But when I got on the train, I sat down and wept. Why? I could remember that back in that town, a dozen people had been prayed for who were not healed at all. They were just as worthy perhaps as the ones who were healed. And, beloved, if Jesus had been down to Pullman instead of Brother Lake, they would all have been healed.

There is a place for you and me, way down at the feet of the Lord Jesus Christ, in humility so deep and true that God can put upon us the real power of God in that holy, heavenly measure that is necessary for the blessing and healing of all men.

Take your umbrellas down. The Spirit is falling. The cry is going up from the souls of men for a new revelation of the power of God through Christ. Bless His name.

Savior? Yes, bless God, Savior from every sin. Do not try to jellyfish your conscience and make yourself believe that you are not sinning, or that there is no sin. No, bless God. There is a power of God so real and true that it will take from your heart every desire for sin and make it so offensive to your soul that your spirit will turn from it. Yes, it will fill you with the Holy Ghost until you rise up a prince and king. Sin gone, sickness gone, the power of God reigning in your life, giving you the glory that was in the face of Jesus, blessed be His name, and putting a song of joy in your heart and the radiant glory of heaven in your life.

Yes, bless God, for this salvation my soul prays, and I pray today that upon this audience the power of God will descend, which will open our consciousness to God and take us into the Holy Ghost and reveal the Christ in us, transforming our nature and making us like Him. Not a little like Him, but in the measure of the stature of the fullness of Christ. (See Ephesians 4:13.) Like Him, like God, like Christ in deed and in truth. God bless you. Amen.

Chapter Twenty-eight

Reality

Sermon

February 11, 1917

For both he that sanctifieth and they who are sanctified are all of one: for which cause he is not ashamed to call them brethren.

(Hebrews 2:11)

When I read the second chapter of Hebrews, there is a thrill that goes down through my soul, and I would to God that the real spiritual truths of it could forever be established in the minds of men.

I once listened to an eminent clergyman preaching from the text, *"What is man?"* (Job 7:17; 15:14). When he got through, I had a feeling that man was a kind of whipped cur [mongrel dog] with his tail between his legs, sneaking out to throw himself into the lake, saying, "Here goes nothing." I said, "He has never caught the fire of the thing Jesus is endeavoring to teach through the writer of Hebrews: that man was the crowning creation of God, that God endowed man with a nature and qualities that, by His grace, can express more of God than any other of God's creations. God purposed by the Holy Spirit to make the salvation of Jesus Christ so real in the nature of man that 'he that sanctifieth [Jesus Christ] and they who are sanctified' through His grace are both of one nature, of one substance, of one character—one in life, one in the righteousness of His death, and one in the consequent dominion that came because of His resurrection and glory."

Brethren of the Lord Jesus Christ. He is the elder brother, and we are the younger members of the family of the same Father, begotten by the same Spirit, energized by the same divine life of God, qualified through the Holy Ghost to perform the same blessed ministry.

He [Jesus] *took not on him the nature of angels; but he took on him the seed of Abraham.*
(Hebrews 2:16)

I wish I could write these things in your soul and brand them in your conscience.

When the purpose of God in the salvation of man first dawned upon my soul—that is, when the greatness of it dawned upon my soul, for experientially, I knew God as Savior from sin—I then knew the power of the Christ within my own heart to keep me above the power of temptation and to help me live a godly life. When I knew the purpose of God and the greatness of His salvation, that is when life became for me a grand new thing.

When by the study of His Word and the revelation of His Spirit it became a fact in my soul that God's purpose was no less in me than it was in the Lord Jesus—and is no less in us as younger brethren than it was in Jesus Christ, our elder brother—then bless God, I saw the purpose that God had in mind for the human race. I saw the greatness of Jesus' desire. That desire that was so intense that it caused Him, as King of Glory, to lay down all the glory He possessed and come to earth to be born as a man, to join hands with our humanity, and by His grace lift us in consciousness and life to the same level that He Himself enjoyed.

Christ became a new factor in my soul. Such a vision of His purpose thrilled my being! I could understand then how it was that, as He approached man and his needs, Jesus began at the very bottom and called mankind to Himself. By His loving touch and the power of the Spirit through His Word, Jesus destroyed the sickness and sin that bound them and set them free in both body and soul, lifting them into union and communion with Himself and God the Father. Yes, bless God, by the Holy Spirit indwelling the souls of men, Christ purposed to bestow on mankind the very conditions of His own life and being and to give to man, through the gifts of the Spirit and the gift of the Spirit, the same blessed ministry to the world that He Himself had enjoyed and exercised.

The old song that we used to sing became new to my heart. Its melody runs through my soul:

Salvation, O the joyful sound,
    In a believer's ear.
It soothes our worries, heals our wounds,
    And drives away our fear.

And lots more, bless God.

I could then understand what was in Charles Wesley's heart when he wrote his famous hymn, "Jesus, Lover of My Soul," and penned its climax, those marvelous verses:

Thou, O Christ, art all I want,
More than all in Thee I find;
Raise the fallen, cheer the faint,
Heal the sick and lead the blind.

Just and holy is Thy name;
I am all unrighteousness;
Vile and full of sin I am.
Thou art full of truth and grace.

Plenteous grace with Thee is found,
Grace to cover all my sin.
Let the healing streams abound;
Make and keep me pure within.

Thou of life the fountain art;
Freely let me take of Thee.
Spring Thou up within my heart;
Rise to all eternity.

The same thing was in the spirit of Isaiah when, in the beautiful thirty-fifth chapter, his exultant soul broke forth in the shout of praise:

He will come and save you. Then the eyes of the blind shall be opened, and the ears of the deaf shall be unstopped. Then shall the lame man leap as an hart, and the tongue of the dumb sing: for in the wilderness shall waters break out, and streams in the desert. (Isaiah 35:4–6)

I could understand then the thrill that must have moved David when he sang: *"Bless the LORD, O my soul, and forget not all his benefits: who forgiveth all thine iniquities; who healeth all thy diseases"* (Psalm 103:2–3).

The vision that has called forth the shouts of praise from the souls of men in all ages is the same vision that stirs your heart and mine today. That vision magnifies the divine reality of the salvation of Jesus Christ by which the greatness of God's purpose is revealed to mankind by the Spirit of the Living One. Man sees himself transformed and lifted and unified with the living Christ through the Holy Ghost so that all the parts and energies and functions of the nature of Jesus Christ are revealed through man unto the salvation of the world. Bless God.

The vision of God's relation to man and man's relation to God is changing the character of Christianity from a whimpering groveler, weeping and wailing its way in tears, to the kingly recognition of union and communion with the living Son of God. Yea, bless God, to the recognition of the real act that the Word of God so vividly portrayed in the lesson I read: *"It became him, for whom are all things, and by whom are all things, in bringing many sons unto glory* [not one son in the world, but in bringing of many sons into the world], *to make the captain of their salvation perfect through sufferings"* (Hebrews 2:10). Blessed be God.

I am glad, bless God, that the Scriptures have dignified us with the marvelous title of "sons of God." I am glad there is such a relation as a "son of God" and that, by His grace, the cleansed soul—cleansed by the precious blood of Jesus Christ, filled and energized by His own kingly Spirit—has also become God's king, God's gentleman in deed and in truth, by the grace of God.

The Spirit of the Lord says within my soul that the kingly nature of the Son of God is purposed to be revealed in the nature of every man, in order that Christ's kingliness may be prevalent in all the world and govern the hearts of mankind, even as it governs the hearts of those who know Him and have entered into His glory.

A Young Man's Testimony

I listened to this young man's testimony on Friday night with a thrill in my soul. I want him to tell you what God has done in him and for him.

I do not know whether I can tell it all or not. I am sure there is a good deal I cannot tell.

When I was a lad of about fourteen years old, I was forced into the mines to work, and I worked a great deal in the water, which brought on rheumatism. I was crippled up for years in my younger days and gradually grew worse. I could walk around, but you could hardly help but notice where I was afflicted. It was in the hips and back.

A great many physicians said there was no relief for me. When I came down here to Spokane and was laboring on anything, I could not stoop down. When I would drop my pick or shovel, I would have to pick it up with my feet and reach for it with my hands.

I came to this meeting last fall, and with one prayer by Brother Lake, I was healed in thirty minutes of rheumatism, which had been a constant torture to me for years.

Later on, I contracted tuberculosis and was examined by the county physician, Dr. Stutz, who advised me that the best thing to do was to go to Edgecliff [a sanatorium, a long-term medical treatment facility in Spokane County]. Also, other physicians said I was very bad and they did not think I could live more than six or eight months unless I went out there right away.

I took the same thing for it. I went to the healing rooms[9] for prayer. Brother Peterson also prayed for me. In three weeks, I went to Dr. Stutz, and he could not find a trace of tuberculosis. I have gained eleven pounds, and I never felt better in my life.

That is a simple story, isn't it? But that story is a revealer of the issue that has probably caused more debate in Christian life than almost any other and of which the world has little understanding. This story shows that the Spirit of God is a living force that takes possession of the nature of man and works in man the will of God, and the will of God is ever to make man like Himself. Blessed be His precious name.

---

[9] For more information about healing rooms and to locate current, ongoing ministries, go to http://healingrooms.com.

It would be a strange world indeed and a strange salvation if Jesus was not able to produce from the whole race one man in His own image, in His own likeness, and of His own character. We would think that salvation was weak, would we not?

If the world were nothing but cripples, as it largely is—soul cripples, physical cripples, mental cripples everywhere—then I want to know what kind of a conception the world has received of the divinity of Jesus Christ, of the power of His salvation. Is there no hope, is there no way out of the difficulty, is there no force that can lift the soul of man into union with God so that once again the life of God thrills in his members?

Our purpose, by the grace of God, is to reveal to the world what is the real truth and purpose and power of the salvation of the Lord Jesus Christ. My soul rejoices every time I see a man set free, for I can say with my whole heart, "Here is one more witness to the divine fact that the Christ of God is a living power, taking possession of the nature of man and transforming man's being into His own image."

The mere fact of our brother's deliverance from suffering and inability to help himself and a possible premature death is a very small matter in itself in comparison with the wonder it reveals to us. The revelation of the power of God at the command of man, to be applied to the destruction of evil—whether spiritual or physical, mental or psychological—shows us Christ's purpose and desire to bring man, by the grace of God, once more into His heavenly estate where he recognizes himself a son of God. Blessed be His name.

Years ago, I found myself like my brother, but crippled worse than he. When my legs grew out of shape and my body became distorted by the common curse of rheumatism, my pastor said, "Brother, you are glorifying God."

And my church said, "Brother, be patient and endure it. Let the sweetness of the Lord possess your soul." And I was good enough to believe it for a long time, until one day, I discovered that it was not the will of God at all, but the will of the dirty, crooked-legged devil that wanted to make me like himself. And then, bless God, everything was changed. I set aside everything and went to Chicago to the only place where I knew then that a man could get healed. I went to John Alexander Dowie's Divine Healing Home at 12th and Michigan Streets, and an old gray-haired man came and laid his hands on me. The power of God went through my being and made my legs straight, and I went out and walked on the street like a Christian.

Do you know that when my legs straightened out, it taught me the beginning of one of the deepest lessons that ever came to my life? It taught me that God does not appreciate a man with crooked legs any more than He does a man with a crooked soul. I saw the abundant power of the gospel of salvation and that it was placed at the disposal of man to remove all the unchristlikeness of his life; if there was unchristlikeness in his body, he could get rid of the curse by coming to God and being made whole. There is just as much unchristlikeness in men's bodies as in men's souls. That which is in the inner life will also be revealed in the outer life. That which is a fact in the mental and psychological realms will become a fact in the physical also. And, bless God, that which is the divine fact of all facts—that the spirit of man and the Spirit of God are of one substance and one nature—will be revealed as his mind and body take on the spiritual power imparted until they, too, become Christlike. Blessed be His holy name.

The Spirit of the Lord speaks within my soul and says:

Within the breast of every man is the divine image of the living God, in whose image and likeness he was made. Sin is a perversion and sickness an impostor, and the grace and power of God through the Holy Ghost delivers man from all bondage of darkness. Man in all his nature then rises into union and communion with God and becomes one with Him in the truest sense—one in the thoughts of God, one

in the aspirations of God, one in the Spirit of
Jesus Christ as the Savior of man. And man
then gives himself to others as a savior by lift-
ing them, by the grace of God, to *the Lamb of
God, which taketh away the sin of the world"*
(John 1:29).

Blessed be His holy name.

Frederick William Faber wrote these words to
this hymn in 1862:

Souls of men, why will ye scatter
Like a crowd of frightened sheep?
Foolish hearts, why will ye wander
From a love so true and deep?

Was there ever kinder Shepherd
Half so gentle, half so sweet,
As the Savior who would have us
Come and gather round His feet?

There's a wideness in God's mercy,
Like the wideness of the sea:
There's a kindness in His justice,
Which is more than liberty.

There is no place where earth's sorrows
Are more felt than up in heaven;
There is no place where earth's failings
Have such kindly judgment given.

There is welcome for the sinner,
And more graces for the good;
There is mercy with the Savior;
There is healing in His blood.

There is plentiful redemption
In the blood that has been shed.
There is joy for all the members
In the sorrows of the Head.

For the love of God is broader
Than the measure of man's mind,
And the heart of the Eternal
Is most wonderfully kind.

But we make His love too narrow
By false limits of our own,
And we magnify its strictness
With a zeal He will not own.

Pining souls, come nearer Jesus,
And O come, not doubting thus,
But with faith that trusts more bravely
His great tenderness for us.

If our love were but more simple,
We should take Him at His word;
And our lives would be all sunshine
In the sweetness of our Lord.

So the divine realities remain—the reality of God, a living power; the divine assistance; the heavenly nature known to every man who enters by the Spirit through the door, Christ Jesus, into a living experience. The man who doubts is the man on the outside. The man on the inside has no questions to settle as the soul who has never been in contact with His life and power does. But Christ invites mankind to enter with Him into the divine knowledge and heavenly union that makes the spirit of man and the Spirit of God to be one in deed and in truth. Bless God!

Man is the most divine reality that God has given in His great creation. Man in the image of God, man renewed by the life of God, filled with the Holy Spirit, revealing and giving forth by the living Spirit, transformed even as He was transformed. Blessed be His name.

God has made us in the truest and highest sense partners and colaborers with our Lord and Savior Jesus Christ. He has not withheld one possibility that was manifested in Jesus from any man. On the contrary, He invites mankind to come forth in the dignity and power of sons of God and, in and with Christ, join in the mighty wonder of the salvation of the world from sin and sickness and the power of death and darkness and hell. Bless God.

Salvation, to my heart, is Christ's glorious reality. Under a tree way back in Canada one night, I knelt and poured out my heart to God and asked Him by His grace to take possession of my life and nature, make me a Christian man, and let me know the power of His salvation. Thus, Christ was born in my soul. Such a joy of God possessed my heart that, for months following, the leaves of the trees seemed to dance and the birds seemed to sing a new song. Blessed be His name.

The difficulty with the church has been that people are induced to confess their sins to Christ and acknowledge Him as Savior, and there they stop. There they petrify, there they wither, and there they die, dry-rotted. I believe that in these phrases I have expressed the real condition that has taken place in 85 percent of professing Christians in the world. Oh, bless God, we never saw Christ's intention that salvation is to be a progressive growth from the moment of being born again. (See Philippians 2:12–13.)

That day long ago, when the glory light of God first shone into my soul, was a glorious day, the best I had ever known to that moment. But, beloved, it would be a sorrowful thing in my life if I was compelled to look back to that day as the best. No, bless God, there were better days than that. There were days when the Lord God took me into His confidence and revealed His nature and revealed His purpose and revealed His love and revealed His ministry. Yes, bless God, there came a day when God once more, in His loving mercy, endowed me with the Spirit of God to be and perform the things that He had planted in my soul and had revealed in His own blessed Word and life.

I invite you to this life of divine reality. I invite you to enter into the Lord Jesus. I invite you to enter into His nature so that you may know Him, for *"no man can say that Jesus is the Lord, but by the Holy Ghost"* (1 Corinthians 12:3). It is through the revelation of the Spirit of Christ in the soul of man that he is privileged to know Jesus as the Lord. Blessed be God. We may know Him as a character in history; we may know Him as the ideal man; we may know Him as the Christ and Savior. But, we do not know Him as the living God who imparts His own nature and life and power to us until we know Him, as the Scripture says, in the Holy Ghost. Bless God!

The person who has felt that the religious life was a dream or a myth or an abstract something that was hard to lay your hands on, an intangible condition, has been mistaken. I bless God. In the bosom of the Living One are the divine realities of God, filling and thrilling the soul of every recipient of the life of the Lord Jesus.

And the Spirit of the Lord once more speaks within my heart and says,

The joys of God and the glories of heaven and the understanding of angelic existence and being are known only to him who is privileged in

211

consciousness to enter that life and realm. God, by His grace, has purposed that man—in his nature and consciousness—shall live in union and communion with our Father God and with the Lord Jesus Christ His Son. We shall come unto the innumerable company of angels and the presence of just men made perfect, and we shall know the power and wonder of the blood of Jesus that speaketh better things than that of Abel. (See Hebrews 12:22–24.)

As Jesus was the Prophet of all prophets, because of the completeness of the union of His nature with God, man in turn becomes the prophet of prophets as his spirit assimilates with the Spirit of the divine One. That man becomes the lover of all lovers, even as Jesus Christ was the lover of all men, thrilling men with the intensity of His affection in the union of spirit with Himself, binding them by the love of His nature as the bond-slaves of Christ forever.

So the Christian draws to himself the love of men, not because he slavishly desires it, but because of the fact that he obeys Christ's divine law:

Give, and it shall be given unto you; good measure, pressed down, and shaken together, and running over, shall men give into your bosom.

(Luke 6:38)

Blessed be God.

I want to tell you that this little church is one of the most loved of all churches in all the world. I want to tell you that more hungry hearts are turned in longing toward this little company of people than to any other group of worshippers in the land. Why? They have heard that God is here, and the longing of the nature of man to know God causes them to turn their hearts and their faces toward the source of heavenly blessing. Shall we give it to them, or will we disappoint them? Shall they receive the blessing of God through our hearts, or will they turn away hungry and dissatisfied? Yes, I know your answer, for I know the answer of the Spirit: *"Give, and it shall be given unto you."* Blessed be God.

The greatest giver is the greatest receiver. He who gives most, receives most—it's God's divine law. The reverse of God's law is always evidenced in the soul of man as selfishness—always getting, always getting, always getting, until the nature contracts and the face distorts and the brain diminishes and the life that God gave to be abundant becomes an abomination that men are compelled to endure.

Chapter Twenty-nine

Remarkable Manifestations of the Spirit in South Africa

Sermon

While ministering at Johannesburg, South Africa, I received an invitation to preach in the City of Pretoria, Transvaal. Consequently, a series of meetings was arranged for. It was my first visit to Pretoria, and the congregation to whom I ministered was a stranger to me. I was entertained at the home of Mr. So-and-so, Hamilton Street. I arrived about three o'clock in the afternoon. About 4:30, a gentleman called and inquired of Mrs. So-and-so if an American stranger was at her house.

She replied, "Yes, Reverend Lake has just arrived this afternoon from Johannesburg." She told him I was an American and had recently come over to Africa. He asked for an interview.

In the course of this interview, he told me that he had been secretary to Dr. Leyds and acting Secretary of State for the old Transvaal government under Paul Kruger, the last Dutch president of the Transvaal Republic. He told me that when the Boer War closed, because of what he considered faithfulness to the cause he had represented, he refused to sign the agreement recognizing the authority of the British, and in consequence he had been blacklisted as an incorrigible.

This prevented him from obtaining employment. His family had been sent to Europe during the war, and he had no money to bring them back. His property and money had all gone in the cause of the Boers, and he was impoverished. He did not have proper clothes to wear nor food to eat sometimes. He said that, notwithstanding these conditions, his soul was consumed with the problems of state and the desire to alleviate the condition of the Boer people and see the people restored to happiness. In the agony of his soul, he had been in the habit of going into one of the mountains for prayer. After several months of this practice, the Lord revealed to him one day that a great deliverance was coming: that a man would arrive in Pretoria from America on a certain date, and could be found at 75 Hamilton Street, at 4:30 PM.

He said, "This is the date, and I have come in response to the direction of the Spirit, as I received it." He welcomed me as a messenger of the Lord and proceeded to give me the details of the revelation as he had received it. His revelation included political changes that were to transpire, a religious revolution that would grow out of my own work, and many events of national importance, which became historic facts during the next few years.

He further gave prophecy in detail of the European war and Britain's part in it. This was in August 1908.

It was only after I had witnessed event after event come to pass that I became deeply impressed with the real significance of his revelation. He told me that the present meeting I was about to conduct in Pretoria would be marked with extraordinary manifestations of the Spirit, that these manifestations of the Spirit would eventuate in a profound impression of the majesty and power of God upon the minds of the people of South Africa and would create a stimulus of faith in God throughout the world in later years.

Our meeting began at a church on Kerk Street in Pretoria on Thursday night. At the close of the first service, the Spirit of God was deeply manifest upon the people. On Friday afternoon when we assembled, the Spirit of God proceeded to work mightily in the people. Many came to God and confessed their sins. Others who already were Christians sought God with profound earnestness for the real, sanctifying power of God in their lives. Some were baptized in the Holy Spirit, their baptism in the Spirit being marked by speaking in tongues under the power of the Spirit and interpretation of these messages by the Spirit, and also by blessed healings of greatly diseased people.

The meetings ran practically without cessation from then until the following Wednesday at 3 AM.

Each service marked a decided increase in the presence and power of God.

On Saturday night, the church was packed. All available standing room was occupied with men standing shoulder to shoulder. The majority of those who were standing were men from the Tattersall Racing Club. Most of them were Jews. They included horsemen of all classes—bookies, jockeys, stablemen, racetrack gamblers, etc.

I was preaching on the subject of the power of God and in a strong spirit was endeavoring to demonstrate that Jesus Christ was the same yesterday, today, and forever, that His power was as great as it ever was, and that the only necessary qualification for touching God for anything was faith in Him. The audience was greatly moved.

At this point, I observed a gentleman with two ladies endeavoring to squeeze through the crowds who were standing in the aisles. I asked the crowd to separate, if possible, and permit the ladies to come through and tried to arrange sitting space for them on the steps of the platform. As they approached, I observed that one of the ladies held her arms perfectly stiff and did not move them at all. By instinct, I knew at once that she was a rheumatic cripple. As she approached me, I said, "What is the reason you do not move your arms?"

She replied, "My shoulders are set from rheumatics."

I said, "How long have they been like that?"

She replied, "Ten years." I inquired if she had been treated by physicians. She replied, "I have been discharged from three hospitals as incurable."

I said, "What hospitals?"

She answered, "Kimberly, Johannesburg, and Pretoria."

Then I addressed the gentleman who accompanied her and said, "Do you know this lady?"

He said, "Yes. She is my sister-in-law."

I said, "Do you know her story to be correct?"

He said, "Absolutely." I asked her what she had come for. She replied, "In the hope that the Lord would heal me."

I inquired, "Do you wish me to pray for you for healing?"

She said, "Yes."

Then, addressing the noisy crowd of men in the aisles and around the doors, I said, "You men never saw Jesus heal a person in your life. You do not know anything about this matter. You have never witnessed an exhibition of the power of God and, therefore, should be considerate enough to keep still, confess your ignorance of such matters, and learn. This is what I want. Select two of your company, let them come and examine this woman and see if her arms are stiff, as she states."

I waited for them to make their selection, and they put forward two men. I have forgotten the name of one of the men at this time, but the name of the other was Mr. Mulluck, a barber, a very intelligent gentleman. His shop was in the market building. I afterward learned he was an American.

They examined the lady critically and found her arms quite immovable, as she had said. Addressing them, I said, "Have you finished your examination, and are you satisfied her condition is as stated?"

They said, "We are."

"Then," I said, "stand back, for I am going to pray for this woman, that the Lord will heal her." Placing my hands on her shoulders, I commanded in the name of Jesus Christ, the Son of God, that this rheumatic devil that bound the woman be cast out and in Christ's name commanded it to go, rebuking it with all the energy of my soul. The power of God lashed through me like a burning fire until the perspiration burst from the woman's face. Then, taking her by the hands, I said, "In the name of Jesus Christ, put your arms up." The right arm went up. Then I said, "In the name of Jesus, put the other arm up, too." She instantly obeyed. Her arms had become free.

As I moved the arm, making the shoulder rotate, I observed that there was a grinding sound in the joint. Addressing the men who had examined her, I said, "You have never heard a dry joint in your life. Come and put your ear to this woman's back while I make her arm move." As they did so, I moved the arm, and the shoulder joints would grind. The oil had not yet returned to the joints.

In the woman's delight, she threw up her hands and praised God and started for the door. The crowd parted for her, and she disappeared, and I did not meet her again for some months.

Another lady arose and came forward, saying, "I wish you would pray for me." I asked her what was the matter, but she did not reply. I bowed my head, saying, "Jesus, show me what is the matter with this woman." Instantly, the Spirit moved my hand down her body from the throat to the stomach, and I prayed for her. She thanked me and sat down.

Later, I learned that her name was Mrs. Ulyate and that she had had a cancer of the stomach. I said to her, "When you came for prayer, why did you not tell me what was the matter with you?"

She said, "I was doubtful whether you were a real man of God or not. I said to myself, 'If he is, then the Lord will show him, and I will not have to tell him what is the matter with me.'" She was perfectly healed. I visited with her and enjoyed the association of the family during the years that followed.

At a later time, her son, a man of twenty, was healed of total deafness in one ear, the result of an eardrum having been absolutely destroyed in an operation. His healing was instantaneous.

THE JABBER FAMILY

On Sunday morning as the service progressed, a gentleman of prominence, who was an employee of the government, came into the meeting, a Mr. Jabber, a man of great statute. As he walked into the church, the Spirit of the Lord fell upon him while he was walking up the aisle, and he fell prostrate on the floor. Several sons were present in the audience, and Mrs. Jabber, his wife, was conducting the choir.

The mother, daughter, and sons gathered from their places in the audience and reverently knelt in a semicircle about him while the audience remained in quiet prayer. The Spirit of the Lord dealt marvelously with him, revealing his sins, and Christ unto salvation.

Presently the Spirit fell upon one of the sons, who fell prostrate by the side of the father, then upon another and another, until the whole family lay prostrate under the power of God. When the Spirit of the Lord had lifted somewhat from them, these sons confessed their disobedience to their parents and to God. And the whole family knelt with their arms around one another, melted by the tenderness of the presence and power of God. Confession and repentance on the part of each to the other made the household of one soul. Words are a poor medium to describe such an event as this. It would have to be seen to be realized. The tenderness and conscious presence of God, the melting power of His mighty Spirit, could only be understood by one who had looked on. No words can tell the story.

Notwithstanding the mighty manifestations of the Spirit, I was anxious that the real working out of the Spirit of God would remove all character of denominational prejudices and those elements in man's nature that keep him from loving and serving God with the broadness in the beauty and grace of holy charity—all that should be utterly removed from the people's hearts.

A PROSTRATE CHOIR

As I was preaching during the afternoon, the Spirit fell on a young lady, Miss Jabber, a cousin of the family aforementioned. She fell from her chair prostrate on the floor, where she remained for a considerable time. The young gentleman who accompanied her and who reverently knelt beside her when she became prostrate was attracted by her desire to speak to him. She said to him, "Send Mr. Lake to me." I ceased preaching and went to her. I asked her what it was she wanted. She said, "Jesus came and talked to me and told me to tell Mr. Lake not to be discouraged, that the power of God will mightily fall upon this meeting tonight."

About four o'clock PM, I left the service and went home to rest. I had been on my feet so long without rest or sleep that it seemed as if I could continue no further. I lay down to nap, saying, "Wake me at 7:30 for the evening service." I fell into a sound sleep, and when it came 7:30, the family reasoned that I was so exhausted, it would be a shame to wake me, and they would endeavor to get through the evening service without my aid.

However, I awoke at 8:00 and hastened to the church. When I arrived, I found that, in view of my absence, the church service was being conducted in their former formal manner instead of the open character of services we had been having. An air of formality pervaded the house. The choir members, about thirty people, were in their places, including the organist, pianist, and director. The choir gallery was arranged with raised steps so that each row of singers sat above the other. The choir chairs were fastened together in sections but were not fastened to the floor.

When I came into the meeting, the pastor who was in charge invited me to preach in his stead. As I preached, my spirit was annoyed by the extreme air of formality that pervaded the meeting, and in my soul I kept praying, "God, do something with this choir. Do something to break up the formality of this service so there may be freedom of the Spirit, so that sinners' hearts may be melted, so that the power of God may descend upon the meeting and the baptism of the Spirit fall."

As this prayer of my soul continued, the Spirit of the Lord suddenly spoke within me, saying, "Go on with your service. I will take care of the choir."

The anointing of the Spirit came upon me, and I spoke with great liberty in the Lord. I was soon so lost in the Spirit that I forgot altogether about the choir, and the formality of the service entirely disappeared. I preached until ten o'clock, when I stepped from the platform and knelt on the floor of the church to pray. An unusual spirit of prayer came upon me, the burden of which was so intense that it caused me to pour out my soul to God in a more than ordinary manner. As I prayed, the Spirit continued to deepen upon me until I was unable to speak in English any longer, and the Spirit caused me to pray in tongues. At such times, the Spirit of the Lord would give me the interpretation of the prayer in English, which would immediately follow the prayer in tongues.

I was lost in prayer but was conscious of a considerable noise. I did not raise my head or open my eyes until the burden of prayer was lifted from my soul. When I looked up, to my amazement, the audience was standing, and at the back of the house, many were standing on their seats, and all were looking toward the choir gallery.

As I turned toward the choir, I saw that the Spirit of the Lord had fallen upon the choir and almost every one of them lay prostrate under the power of the Spirit. When they fell from their seats, they pushed the chairs on the row in front of them forward, so that the front legs of the chairs dropped over the edge of the narrow platform. The whole row would turn upside down on top of those who had already fallen prostrate in front.

The deacons of the church came and gathered the chairs off of the prostrate ones as quickly as possible. The unbelievers in the house were startled and frightened at this manifestation; they arose and rushed out of the door. I instructed the doorkeeper to turn the key in the door and not permit anyone to come in. The awe of God overshadowed the house. I felt it was not time for unbelievers to be present. God wanted to deal with the church.

I went and sat down in the audience. We remained perfectly quiet in prayer for some time. Then, one after another of the prostrate ones began to pray and confess his waywardness and sin to God. There seemed to be but one passion in their souls, to tell out to God the burden of their unbelief, of their sin, their backslidings, and to call on God for forgiveness and restoration and power to overcome. As a soul would thus confess out and pray through into the presence of God, the Spirit of the Lord would lift from him, and he would be permitted to arise. As he did so, he was in a perfectly normal state of mind, excepting that the awe of God's presence and power was mightily realized by each.

Many sat and wept. Others sang for joy. Many were baptized in the Holy Spirit. One young man among the tenor singers lay on the lower platform. Close to him was his sweetheart, a young lady who was a member of the church. Like the others, he was pouring out the confession of his life to God, and to her, telling of his peculiar sins, which were many and vile. Husbands were confessing to wives and wives to husbands, children to their parents, sweethearts to sweethearts, and all to God.

The pianist, Mr. Braun, lay beside the piano stool for possibly an hour, helpless and speechless, as the Spirit of God worked in him. I was moved by the Spirit of God to go to him and pray. As I knelt beside him, my hands involuntarily moved to his chest, and laying my hands on him, I prayed. I did not know why I did so. I just obeyed the guidance of the Spirit. As I prayed, I was conscious of the Spirit of God flowing through me to him.

I returned to my seat, and in about half an hour, he began to pour out his heart to God. When he had finished, he motioned me to come to him. When I reached him, he said, "Send my wife to me." I went to the back of the house, where his wife sat weeping, and brought her to him. She knelt beside him. He put his arms about her and confessed that for three years he had been living in adultery. They wept together for hours. God worked so mightily in them that at three or four in the morning, they returned to their home, praising God together.

The next day at ten o'clock, he called on me to tell me that the Lord had baptized both him and his wife in the Holy Spirit and that when they were baptized, the Spirit of God came upon both and caused them to speak in tongues and praise God in a spirit of prophecy. His soul was aglow.

He said, "When you prayed for me last night, why did you put your hands on my chest?"

I replied, "I do not know. I simply obeyed the impulse of the Spirit."

He asked, "Did you know I was sick and needed healing?"

I said, "No, I did not know it."

"Well," he said, "I want to show you what the Lord has done." And he opened his clothing and showed me a cancer on the chest, saying, "Three years ago when

I went into adultery, this cancer appeared on my body within a few days. I have endeavored to hide it from everyone. Even my wife did not know of its existence; no one but my physician knew. But look at it now. See how the power of God has withered it?" It had turned brown as if burned by a fire, and in a few days, it utterly disappeared.

Among other things, the Spirit of the Lord directed Mr. Braun to make restitution to parties with whom he had had dishonest dealings at different times. One that I especially remember was this: he was employed by the government as a civil engineer on a monthly salary. He had been in the practice at intervals of filling out a report saying that he was sick and unable to attend to his duties and would be gone for some days. He was compelled to confess to his superiors that this was not a fact and that he used this time in recreation.

The thoroughness with which God dealt with each and all of these was very remarkable. Lives were cleansed to the very inmost, every sin, both outward and secret. The Spirit of God had taken possession, and natures were changed into the likeness and nature of Jesus Christ.

These meetings were the beginning of a mighty work of God at Pretoria, which continues to this day.

Chapter Thirty

The Spirit of God

Sermon

I want to read to you one of the best incidents in the Word of God. It is the story of Elijah upon Mount Carmel.

And it came to pass, when Ahab saw Elijah, that Ahab said unto him, Art thou he that troubleth Israel? And he answered, I have not troubled Israel; but thou, and thy father's house, in that ye have forsaken the commandments of the LORD, and thou hast followed Baalim. Now therefore send, and gather to me all Israel unto mount Carmel, and the prophets of Baal four hundred and fifty, and the prophets of the groves four hundred, which eat at Jezebel's table.

So Ahab sent unto all the children of Israel, and gathered the prophets together unto mount Carmel. And Elijah came unto all the people, and said, How long halt ye between two opinions? if the LORD be God, follow him: but if Baal, then follow him. And the people answered him not a word. Then said Elijah unto the people, I, even I only, remain a prophet of the LORD; but Baal's prophets are four hundred and fifty men. Let them therefore give us two bullocks;

and let them choose one bullock for themselves, and cut it in pieces, and lay it on wood, and put no fire under: and I will dress the other bullock, and lay it on wood, and put no fire under: and call ye on the name of your gods, and I will call on the name of the LORD: and the God that answereth by fire, let him be God. And all the people answered and said, It is well spoken.

And Elijah said unto the prophets of Baal, Choose you one bullock for yourselves, and dress it first; for ye are many; and call on the name of your gods, but put no fire under. And they took the bullock which was given them, and they dressed it, and called on the name of Baal from morning even until noon, saying, O Baal, hear us. But there was no voice, nor any that answered. And they leaped upon the altar which was made. And it came to pass at noon, that Elijah mocked them, and said, Cry aloud: for he is a god; either he is talking, or he is pursuing, or he is in a journey, or peradventure he sleepeth, and must be awaked. And they cried aloud, and cut themselves after their manner with knives and lancets, till the blood gushed out upon them. And it came to pass, when midday was past, and they prophesied until the time of the offering of the evening sacrifice, that there was neither voice, nor any to answer, nor any that regarded. And Elijah said unto all the

*people, Come near unto me. And all the people
came near unto him. And he repaired the altar
of the LORD that was broken down. And Elijah
took twelve stones, according to the number of
the tribes of the sons of Jacob, unto whom the
word of the LORD came, saying, Israel shall be
thy name: and with the stones he built an altar
in the name of the LORD: and he made a trench
about the altar, as great as would contain two
measures of seed. And he put the wood in order,
and cut the bullock in pieces, and laid him on
the wood, and said, Fill four barrels with water, and pour it on the burnt sacrifice, and on
the wood. And he said, Do it the second time.
And they did it the second time. And he said,
Do it the third time. And they did it the third
time. And the water ran round about the altar;
and he filled the trench also with water. And it
came to pass at the time of the offering of the
evening sacrifice, that Elijah the prophet came
near, and said, LORD God of Abraham, Isaac,
and of Israel, let it be known this day that thou
art God in Israel, and that I am thy servant,
and that I have done all these things at thy
word. Hear me, O LORD, hear me, that this people may know that thou art the LORD God, and
that thou hast turned their heart back again.
Then the fire of the LORD fell, and consumed the
burnt sacrifice, and the wood, and the stones,
and the dust, and licked up the water that was*

in the trench. And when all the people saw it, they fell on their faces: and they said, The LORD, he is the God; the LORD, he is the God. And Elijah said unto them, Take the prophets of Baal; let not one of them escape. And they took them: and Elijah brought them down to the brook Kishon, and slew them there.

(1 Kings 18:17–40)

In every land, among every people, throughout all history, there have been occasions when a demonstration of the power of God was just as necessary to the world as it was in the days of Elijah. It is necessary now.

The people had turned away from God. They had forgotten that there was a God in Israel. They were trusting in other gods, just as the people are today. If I were to call you heathen, I suppose most people would be offended, but I want to say that there is no person with more gods than the average American. Men are bowing down to the god of popularity. Men are bowing down to this god and that god. Men are afraid of the opinion of their neighbors, as any heathen ever was in any time in the world. There is practically no Christian, let alone an unbeliever, who has the real stamina to stand forth and declare his absolute convictions concerning Jesus Christ, the Son of God. Less and less do men have the necessary stamina to declare their convictions as to Jesus Christ, the Savior of mankind.

That is the reason that the modern church has lost her touch with God and has gone into a sleep unto death, a sleep that can only end in spiritual death and the disintegration of the church as she stands. The only power that will revive the church in this land and the world is that which she will receive when she throws her heart open to God, as the people of Israel did, and says, "Lord God, we have sinned."

The sin the church needs to repent of is not the committing a lot of little acts that men call sin, which are the outgrowth of what is in the heart, but the thing that mankind needs to repent of is this: that they have denied the power of God. They have denied to mankind that the Christ of Israel is the Son of God and that He is the almighty Savior. God's call to the Christian churches today is to come forth from their hiding places, just as Elijah came forth, and meet the King. Declare the ground on which you meet the enemies of God, and meet them in the name of Jesus Christ.

The Christian church is absolutely, solely, and entirely to blame for the whole existence of metaphysical associations that are covering the earth like a plague of lice. The church is to blame, for if the church of Jesus Christ for the last fifty or a hundred years had declared to mankind in the power of the Spirit the Christ of Nazareth as He is, there never would have come into existence the whole tribe of metaphysical societies.

The world today is being taken by the metaphysical associations to such an extent that they are bowing before the metaphysical laws and calling them God. That is human nature and not God. The time has come when the Christian church has got to give a new demonstration to the world. If metaphysicians, through the operation of natural laws, can produce a certain character and degree of healing, then it is up to the church of Jesus Christ and the ministry of the Son of God to demonstrate that there is a power in the blood of Jesus Christ to save men and heal men unto the *uttermost*—not half-healed or half the people healed. But I pray and believe that God's time has come for God's challenge to mankind and the challenge of the Christian church to the world is to come on, and if it is God, *let the fire fall.*

There was no bluffing with the old Israelite prophets. When the people came, they laid their sacrifices on the altar, and they did not put artificial fire under it. But instead, the soul went down before God. He lifted his heart to heaven, and then the fire came down and consumed the sacrifice: that was the evidence that the sacrifice was accepted.

The time has come when God wants the fire to fall, and if you, my beloved brother and sister, will pay God's price and make Christ's consecration of yourself to God, we will see God's fire fall. And it will not be destructive, either, except that sin and selfishness and sickness will wither under that fire, while purity and life and holiness and character will stand forth, purified and refined by the glory and the power of the God-fire that comes from heaven. God's fire is creative of righteousness as well as destructive of sin.

Some years ago, when I opened my work in South Africa and the Lord had moved marvelously for about six months, a movement was put on foot to congregate a crowd of Indian Yogis. (The Indian Yogis are a society of people who utterly give themselves up to a demonstration of metaphysical things.) They were Brahman priests, Buddhist priests, Confucian priests, and all kinds of priests and hypnotists. After a time, they said, "We would like to have a demonstration."

And I said, "Yes, I would like to have a demonstration also. Come on with your Yogis and your Buddhas and your Confucians and hypnotists. Let them show their gods. Let them heal people, if they can. Let it be in public, and let it be done on the platform of my tabernacle or any other place large enough to accommodate the public. Then, when you have finished, we will call on the Christian's God and see what He will do."

Well, they came to the tabernacle to make the demonstration. One man, Professor Henerson, a professional hypnotist, was put forward. He said he was there to demonstrate what he could do through hypnotism. He brought with him as his subject a woman from Germiston who had a locked hip, probably from rheumatics of hip disease. After he had tried and tried privately for months and now publicly before the people, I said, "Stand off."

Calling one of the brethren to pray with me, I said, "In the name of the Lord Jesus Christ, I command this hip to become unlocked." Instantly she was healed and walked. I want to tell you more of what God did. That was as far as my faith reached, but God met me at that point. As I stood looking at her, I thought to myself, *That is the way Jesus did it when He was on the earth, and that is the way Jesus does it yet.* It was Jesus who did it.

Well, as I stood looking at her, suddenly something came upon my soul from heaven. It was the anointing of the Spirit of God. I understood then what the blessed Good Book talked about when it spoke of the Spirit of the Lord coming upon Elijah[10] and the Spirit of the Lord coming upon Samson (see Judges 14:6, 19, and 15:14), etc. Samson, under the power of the Spirit, took the gates of Gaza and carried them off. (See Judges 16:30.) He took the jawbone of an ass and killed a thousand men with it. (See Judges 15:15.) These were the things by which God endeavored to teach the world what the Spirit of the Lord is.

Well, as I stood there, the Spirit fell upon me, not like the gentle dew of heaven but in power, until

---

[10] 1 Kings 18:46 says the "*hand of the LORD*" was upon Elijah.

my spirit towered up in such strength that I did not know how to control it. In my heart, I cried out, "My God, what does it mean?" All at once, I discovered the Spirit going out in operation to the spirit of that hypnotist. I said, "Are you the man who has been hypnotizing this woman for two years and grafting her hard-earned money? In the name of Jesus Christ, you will never hypnotize anyone else." Grasping him by the coat front, I struck him on the shoulder with my other hand, saying, "In the name of the Son of God, come out of him." And it came out. That hypnotic demon was gone out of him. He never hypnotized again but earned an honest living.

God is not the God of the dead. He is the God of the living. And the desire in my soul is that in this city, God Almighty would raise up an altar unto the living God, not unto a dead God. Mankind needs an altar to the living God, to the God that hears prayer, to the God that answers prayer, to the God that answers by fire. The time has come when God's challenge has gone forth. God is saying, "If there is a Christian, let him pray. If there is a God, let Him answer." God will meet the souls every time you turn to Him and meet Him face-to-face.

In emphasizing this, the Lord Jesus Christ says to the world, *"What things soever ye desire, when ye pray, believe that ye receive them, and ye shall have them"* (Mark 11:24). That is what the matter is. Your blank check is not worth ten cents in your hands. Why? Because you do not believe God. Fill in your check, believe God, and it will come to pass.

The call of Elijah is the call of the present hour. If the Christ is the Christ, get your answer from Him. If Jesus is the Son of God with power on the earth to forgive sins, then, as Jesus put it,

> *But that ye may know that the Son of man hath power upon earth to forgive sins,...I say unto thee, Arise, and take up thy couch, and go into thine house.* [Get up and walk.]   (Luke 5:24)

Jesus Christ was reasonable enough to meet man's reasoning and inquiries. And the minister of God who is afraid to walk out and believe his God and trust his God for results is no Christian at all.

What does Christianity mean to the world? Is it a hope for the glory land way off in the future? Is that Christianity? Is it a hope that you are not going to fry in hell all the days of your life? No! Christianity is the demonstration of the righteousness of God to the world.

So, brethren, God has given us something to do. He has given us a demonstration to make. If we do not make it, then we have no more right to the claims that we make of being sons of God than other people. If God be God, serve Him; if Baal, then serve him.

Chapter Thirty-one

The Baptism of the Holy Ghost

Sermon Series

Sermon 1 of 3 • February 23, 1921

The baptism of Holy Ghost is the greatest event in Christian history—greater than the crucifixion, of greater import than the resurrection, greater than the ascension, greater than the glorification. It was the end and finality of crucifixion and resurrection, ascension and glorification.

If Jesus Christ had been crucified and there had been no resurrection, His death would have been without avail, insofar as the salvation of mankind is concerned. Or, if He had risen from the grave in resurrection and failed to reach the throne of God and receive from the Father the gift of the Holy Ghost, the purpose for which He died and for which He arose would have been missed.

It is because there was no failure. It is because Jesus went to the ultimate, to the very throne and heart of God, and secured the almighty Spirit right out of the heavenly treasury of the Eternal Soul and poured it forth upon the world in divine baptism, that we are here tonight.

BIRTHDAY OF CHRISTIANITY

The day of Pentecost was the birthday of Christianity. Christianity never existed until the Holy Ghost came from heaven. The ministry of Jesus in the world was His own divine preparation of the world for His ultimate and final ministry. His ultimate and final ministry was to be *by the Spirit.*

The ministry of Jesus during His earthly life was localized by His humanity and localized again in that His message was only given to Israel. But the descent of the Holy Ghost brought to the souls of men a *universal* ministry of Jesus to every man, right from the heart of God. Heavenly contact with the eternal God in power set their nature all aflame for God and with God, exalted their natures into God, and made the recipient *godlike.* Man became godlike!

HOLY GROUND

There is no subject in all the Word of God that seems to me should be approached with so much holy reverence as the subject of the baptism of the Holy Ghost. Beloved, my heart bleeds every day of my life when I hear the flippancy with which Christians discuss the baptism of the Holy Ghost.

When Moses entered into the presence of God at the burning bush, God said, *"Put off thy shoes from off thy feet, for the place whereon thou standest is holy ground"* (Exodus 3:5). How much more so when the individual comes into the presence of God looking for the baptism of the Holy Ghost and remembers that in order to obtain this gift, Jesus Christ lived in the world, bled on the cross, entered into the darkness of death and hell and the grave, grappled with and strangled that accursed power, came forth again, and finally ascended to heaven in order to secure it for you and me. If there is anything under heaven that ought to command our reverence, our holy reverence, our reverence beyond anything else in the world, it surely is the subject of the baptism of the Holy Ghost.

My! Sometimes my soul is jarred when I hear people flippantly say, "Have you got your baptism?" Supposing that Jesus was on the cross and we were privileged tonight to look into His face at this hour, I wonder, what would the feeling of our souls be? Supposing we were to follow tonight behind the weeping company that bore His dead body and laid it in the tomb, what would our feelings be? Supposing we were to meet Him in the garden, as Mary did, in the glory of His resurrection, or supposing that God in His goodness would let us look into that scene of scenes at the throne of God, when the heavens lifted up their gates and the Lord of Glory came in. Oh, if we could, beloved, we would have a better comprehension of the baptism of the Holy Ghost.

I love that dear, old word, "Ghost." The Anglo-Saxon is *Ghest*—a spiritual guest, heavenly visitor, spiritual presence, the Angel One. And the Angel One who comes to you and me comes right out of the heart of the eternal God, breathed through the soul of Jesus Christ! When the Holy Ghost came upon a man originally, as He did upon the hundred and twenty at Jerusalem, no one went around saying, "Brother, have you got your baptism?" They were walking with their shoes off, with uncovered heads and uncovered hearts before the eternal God!

I believe that the first essential in a real Holy Ghost church and a real Holy Ghost work is to begin to surround the baptism of the Holy Ghost with that due reverence of God with which an experience so sacred and that cost such an awful price should be surrounded.

A LESSON ON REVERENCE

I sat one day on a kopje in South Africa in company with a lady, Mrs. Dockrall, a beautiful woman of God, baptized in the Holy Ghost. As we sat together on the rocks, meditating and praying, the rest of the company being a little distance away, I observed the Spirit falling upon her powerfully, until she was submerged in the Spirit. Then she began to deliver a message, first in tongues, later giving the interpretation in English, and I listened to the most wonderful lecture on the subject of reverence I have ever heard in all my life.

Afterward I said to her, "Tell me what you can about the experience through which you have just passed."

She had never been in Europe, but she said, "I was carried by the Spirit somewhere in Europe. I approached a great cathedral." And she went on to describe its architecture. She said, "As I approached the door, I was greeted by an English priest who led me down the aisle to the altar, and I knelt. A white cloud began to settle down, and presently out of the cloud came the face and form of Jesus Christ. The priest was standing in the rostrum and began to speak, but I could see by the action of the Spirit that the words he spoke were simply words that were being spoken by the Lord."

It has always been one of the sorrows of my life that I did not have a stenographer who could have recorded that wonderful message on reverence for the works of God.

I have been reading one of the most beautiful books I have ever read. It is written by an English lady, Mrs.

Parker, a missionary to India, and describes the life and teaching and mission of one Sadhu Sundar Singh, an Indian sadhu. A sadhu is a holy man who renounces the world absolutely and utterly, never marries, never takes part in any of the affairs of the world, separates himself to religious life, and practices meditation on God and the spiritual life. Sundar Singh, when he found the Lord Jesus Christ, conceived the idea of becoming a Christian sadhu. He walked from place to place. He wore no shoes, and he slept on the ground, but his life is utterly abandoned to God.

One of the statements of Mrs. Parker, who wrote of Sundar Singh, was to this effect: "As you approach his presence, an awe comes over the soul. It seems as if you are again in the presence of the original Nazarene." Let us approach the Holy of Holies with a similar awe. Let us be reverential in the presence of the Glorified One.

The baptism of the Holy Ghost is peculiar to the Lord Jesus Christ. John the Baptist said,

I indeed baptize you with water unto repentance: but he that cometh after me is mightier than I, whose shoes I am not worthy to bear: he shall baptize you with the Holy Ghost, and with fire: whose fan is in his hand, and he will thoroughly purge his floor, and gather his wheat into the garner; but he will burn up the chaff with unquenchable fire.

(Matthew 3:11–12)

Jesus Christ, the Glorified, must lay His hands on you and on me and bestow upon us all His own nature, the outflow of God, the substance of His soul, the quality of His mind, the very being of God Himself. *"Know ye not that your body is the temple of the Holy Ghost which is in you?"* (1 Corinthians 6:19). A temple of God, a house of God in which God lives!

A HABITATION OF GOD

Sometimes I have tried to get it clear before my soul that God *lives in me*. I have tried to note the incoming influence and power of that pure, sweet, living Spirit of the eternal God. I have tried to realize His presence in my spirit, in my soul, in my hands, in my feet, in my person and being—a habitation of God, a habitation of God! God, equipping the soul to minister Himself to the world; God, equipping the soul of man so that he may live forever in harmony of mind with God; God, finishing to the soul of man the power of His personality, by which man is made as God—all the godlike qualities of your heart are due to the fact that God by the Spirit dwells in you. What is it that you look for in another? It is God. You look into the eyes of another to see God. If you fail to see God in the other life, your heart is troubled. You were looking for God.

I am not interested in the form or the figure or the name of an individual. I am interested in seeing

God. Is God there? Is God in that man? Is God in that woman? Is it God who speaks? Is it God who moves? Are you seeing God?

YOU MAY HAVE GOD

The baptism of the Holy Ghost was the *incoming* of God into a personality in order that the man, through this force, might be moved by God. God lives in him; God speaks through him; God is the impulse of his soul; God has His dwelling place in him.

You may have God. That is the wonder of the baptism of the Holy Ghost. It is not a work of grace; it is God *possessing you.* Oh, your heart may have been as sinful as the heart of man ever was sinful. But Christ comes to your soul. That spirit of darkness that possessed you goes, and in its stead, a new Spirit comes in, the Spirit of Christ. You have become a new creature, a saved man, a God-filled man.

A TRANSFORMATION

Sin manifests itself in three ways: in thought, in act, and in nature. Salvation is a complete transformation. God takes possession of man and changes his thoughts; in consequence, his acts change, and his nature is new. A Christian is not a reformed man.

A Christian is a man renewed, remade by the Spirit of God. A Christian is a man indwelt by God—the house of God, the tabernacle of the Most High! Man, indwelt by God, becomes the hands and the heart and the feet and the mind of Jesus Christ. God descends into man; man ascends into God! That is the purpose and power of the baptism in the Holy Ghost. A soul is saved. How does Jesus reach them? Through your hands, through your heart, through your faith. When God baptizes you in the Holy Ghost, He gives you the biggest gift that heaven or earth ever possessed. He gives you *Himself!* He joins you by the Spirit to Himself forever.

THE REQUIREMENT

The requirement is a surrendered heart, a surrendered mind, a surrendered life. From the day that a man becomes a child of God, baptized in the Holy Ghost, it was God's intention through Jesus Christ that man should be a revelation of Jesus.

If you were looking to know whether a man was baptized in the Holy Ghost or not, what would you look for? You would look for God in him. You would look for a revelation of the personality of God—God moving in him, God speaking in him, God speaking through him, God using his hands, God using his feet; a mind in harmony with God, a soul in touch with heaven, a spirit united and unified with and in Jesus Christ.

GOD'S GREAT PURPOSE NOT COMPREHENDED

It is not in my heart to discourage any man or to make you disbelieve for one minute in the trueness of your own baptism in the Holy Ghost. I believe that God, by the Spirit, has baptized many in the Holy Ghost. Hundreds and hundreds of people have been baptized in the Holy Ghost during the life of this church in the last six years. But, beloved, we have not comprehended the greatness of God's intent—not that we have not received the Spirit, but our lives have not been sufficiently surrendered to God. We must keep on ascending right to the throne, right into the heart of God, right into the soul of the Glorified.

THE HOLY GHOST, A GIFT OF GOD HIMSELF

The common teaching that my heart these days is endeavoring to combat is that God comes to present the individual with a gift of power, and the individual is then supposed to go out and manifest some certain characteristic of power. No! God comes to present you with Himself: *"Ye shall receive power, **after** that the Holy Ghost is come upon you"* (Acts 1:8).

Jesus went to heaven in order that the very treasury of the heart of the eternal God might be unlocked for your benefit, that out of the very soul of the eternal God, the streams of His life and nature would possess you from the crown of your head to the soles of your feet, and that there would be just as much of the eternal God in your toenails and in your brain as each is capable of containing. In other words, from the very soles of your feet to the last hair on the top of your head, every cell of your being would be a residence of the Spirit of the living God. Man is made alive by God and with God by the Spirit. And in the truest sense, man is the dwelling place of God, the house of God, the tabernacle of the Most High.

Listen! *"The words that I speak unto you I speak not of myself: but the Father that dwelleth in me"* (John 14:10). *"But the Father that dwelleth in me."* Where did the eternal Father dwell in Jesus Christ? Why, in every part of His being, within and without in the spirit of Him, in the soul of Him, in the brain of Him, in the body of Him, in the blood of Him, in the bones of Him! Every single, solitary cell of His structure was the dwelling place of God, of God, of God!

When you look for God, you do not look on the surface. You look within. When you discern a man to see whether God is in him, you look into the spirit of him, into the soul of him, into the depths of him, and there you see God.

How trifling are the controversies that surround the baptism of the Holy Ghost. Men are debating such trifling issues. For instance, does a man speak in tongues or does he not? Do you think for a moment that I am discounting the value of tongues? I am not. But, beloved, I will tell you what my heart is straining for. Down there at Jerusalem, they not only spoke in tongues, but they spoke the *languages of the nations.* (See Acts 2:6–11.)

If it was possible for Peter and Paul or for the Jewish nation, then it is possible for every last one of us. Not to speak in tongues alone, as we ordinarily understand that phrase, but to speak because God dwells in us and speaks to whomever He will in whatever language He desires. And if your present experience in tongues is not satisfying, God bless you; go on into languages, as God meant that you should. Dear ones, I feel the need of that, and I feel it way down in my heart to a depth that hurts. I lived in South Africa for a number of years, where it is commonly said that there are a hundred thousand tribes of native people. Every last one of the hundred thousand speaks a different dialect. These tribes sometimes number as low as ten thousand people and sometimes as high as hundreds of thousands, even millions of people.

Suppose we were going to undertake to evangelize Africa rapidly. It would be necessary to have a hundred thousand different missionaries and have them all at one time master one particular language each, for there are a hundred thousand of them. No sir! I believe before high heaven that when the Spirit of the eternal God is poured out upon all flesh, that out of the real Christian body will arise a hundred thousand men and women in Africa that will speak in the language of every separate tribe by the power of God.

The unknown tongue of the Spirit was to teach you of God, to be a faith builder in your soul, to take you into God's big, practical endeavor to save the world. And that is the reason, dear ones, that I bring this issue to your souls tonight. In the matter of the baptism of the Holy Ghost, we are in a state of the merest infancy of understanding, the merest infancy of divine control, the merest infancy of ability to assimilate into our environment, including languages.

When we go to a school, we see classes arranged for every grade. I was talking to a young schoolteacher who teaches out in the country in a little public school. I said, "How many children have you in your school?"

She replied "Fifteen."

I asked, "How many grades have you?"

She said, "Eight grades." Fifteen scholars divided into eight grades.

The Christian church is God's big school. What student in the eighth grade would think of saying to the child learning his ABCs: "You haven't anything. Why don't you have the eighth grade understanding?" Well, he will have it in due time. That is the reason the student does not say it. It is because he knows the child will have it. One day, that boy will understand just the same as he does. A weak Christianity always wants to drop to the imperfect and adjust itself to the popular mind, but real Christianity ever seeks to be made perfect in God, both in character and gifts.

MY PERSONAL EXPERIENCE

Dear ones, I want to repeat to you tonight a little of my own personal history on the subject of the baptism of the Spirit, for I know it will clarify your soul.

MY CONVERSION

I knelt under a tree when about sixteen years of age in repentance and prayer, and God came into my soul. I was saved from my sins, and from that day, I knew Jesus Christ as a living Savior. There never was a single moment of question about the reality of

His coming into my life as a Savior, for He saved me from my sins. My friend said, "You are baptized in the Holy Ghost."

SANCTIFIED

Sometime later, I think when I was yet under twenty or thereabouts, I met a Christian farmer, Melvin Pratt, who sat down on his plow handles and taught me the subject of sanctification, and God let me enter into that experience. My friends said, "Now surely you are baptized in the Holy Ghost."

Later in my life, I came under the ministry of George B. Watson of the Christian and Missionary Alliance, who taught the baptism of the Holy Ghost and sanctification with more clarity and better distinction between the two, and I entered into a richer life and a better experience. A beautiful anointing of the Spirit was upon my life.

MINISTRY OF HEALING

Then the ministry of healing was opened to me, and I ministered for ten years in the power of God. Hundreds and hundreds of people were healed by the power of God during this ten years, and I could feel the conscious flow of the Holy Spirit through my soul and my hands.

But at the end of that time, I believe I was the hungriest man for God who ever lived. There was such a hunger for God that, as I left my offices in Chicago and walked down the street, my soul would break out, and I would cry, "Oh God!" I have had people stop and look at me in wonder. It was the yearning passion of my soul, asking for God in a greater measure than I then knew. But my friends would say, "Mr. Lake, you have a beautiful baptism in the Holy Ghost." Yes, it was nice as far as it went, but it was not answering the cry of my heart. I was growing into a larger understanding of God and my own soul's need. My soul was demanding a greater entrance into God, His love, His presence, and His power.

MY BAPTISM IN THE HOLY GHOST

And then one day, an old man strolled into my office, sat down, and in the next half hour revealed more of the knowledge of God to my soul than I had ever known before. And when he left, I said, "God bless that old, gray head. That man knows more of God than any man I ever met. By the grace of God, if that is what the baptism of the Holy Ghost with tongues does, I am going to possess it." Oh, the wonder of God that was then revealed to my heart!

I went into fasting and prayer and waiting on God for nine months. Then, one day, the glory of God came to my life in a new manifestation and a new incoming. And when the phenomena had passed, and the glory of it remained in my soul, I found that my life began to manifest in the varied range of the gifts of the Spirit, and I spoke in tongues by the power of God, and God flowed through me with a new force. Healings were of a more powerful order. Oh, God lived in me, God manifested in me, God spoke through me! My spirit was deified, and I had a new comprehension of God's will, new discernment of spirit, new revelation of God in me.

For nine months, everything that I looked at framed itself into poetic verse. I could not look at the trees without the scene framing itself into a glorious poem of praise. I preached to audiences of thousands night after night and day after day. People came from all over the world to study me. They could not understand. Everything I said was a stream of poetry. It rolled from my soul in that form. My spirit had become a fountain of poetic truth.

Then, a new wonder was manifested. My nature became so sensitized that I could lay my hands on any man or woman and tell what organ was diseased and to what extent and all about it. I tested it. I went to hospitals where physicians could not diagnose a case, touched a patient, and instantly I knew the organ that was diseased, its extent and condition and location. And one day the gift passed away. A child gets to playing with a toy, and his joy is so wonderful that he sometimes forgets to eat.

Oh, say, don't you remember when you were first baptized in the Holy Ghost and you first spoke in tongues, how you bubbled and babbled? It was so wonderful, so amazing. We just wanted to be babies and go on bubbling and exhilarating. And now we are wondering what the matter is. The effervescence seems to have passed away. My! It is a good thing that it did. God is letting your soul down, beloved, into the bedrock, right down where your mind is not occupied anymore with the manifestation of God. God is trying to get your mind occupied with Himself. God has come into you, and now He is drawing you into Himself.

Will you speak in tongues when you are baptized in the Holy Ghost? Yes, you will, but you will do an awful lot more than that, bless God, an awful lot more than that! You will speak with the soul of Jesus Christ. You will feel with the heart of the Son of God. Your heart will beat with a heavenly desire to bless the world, because it is the pulse of Jesus that is throbbing in your soul. And I do not believe there will be a bit of inclination in your heart to turn around to another child of God and say, "You are not in my class. I am baptized with the Holy Ghost." That is as foreign to the Spirit of the Son of God as night is from day. Beloved, if you are baptized in the Holy Ghost, there will be a tenderness in your soul so deep that you will never crush the aspiration of another by a single suggestion, but your soul will throb and beat and pulse in love, and your heart will be under that one to lift him up to God and push him out as far into the glory as your faith can send it.

I want to talk with the utmost frankness and say to you that tongues have been to me the making of my ministry. It is that peculiar communication with God when God reveals to my soul the truth I utter to you day by day in my ministry. But that time of communication with me is mostly in the night. Many a time, I climb out of bed, take my pencil and pad, and jot down the beautiful, wonderful things of God that He talks out in my spirit and reveals to my heart.

Many Christians do not understand the significance of tongues any more than the other man understands the experience of your soul when you are saved from sin. It has taken place in you. It is in your heart, it is in your mind, it is in your being. The man who tries to make you doubt the reality of your touch with God when He saved you out of your sin is foolish. It is established *in* you. The old Methodists could not explain the experience, but they said, "It is better felt than told." They knew it by internal knowledge. So it is in a real baptism of the Holy Ghost. So it is in prophecy. So it is in healing. So it is in tongues. Do not throw away what you have. Go on to perfection.

THE LANGUAGE OF THE SPIRIT

The spirit of man has a voice. Do you get that? The spirit of man has a voice. The action of God in your spirit causes your spirit to speak by its voice. In order to make it intelligent to your understanding, it has to be repeated in the language that your brain knows. Why? Because there is a language common to the spirit of man, and it is not English and it is not German and it is not French and it is not Italian or any other of the languages of earth. It is a language of the spirit of man. And, oh, what a joy it was when that pent-up, bursting, struggling spirit of yours found its voice and *"began to speak with other tongues, as the Spirit gave...utterance"* (Acts 2:4).

Many a time I have talked with others in the Spirit, by the Spirit, through the medium of tongues, and comprehended everything that was said to me, but I did not know it with my rational mind. It was not the sound of their words. It was that indefinable something that made it intelligent to my spirit. Spirit speaks to spirit, just as man speaks to man. Your spirit speaks to God. God is Spirit. He answers back. Bless God! And I believe with all my heart that is what Paul had in mind when he talked about the "unknown" tongue. (See 1 Corinthians 14.) The unknown tongue is that medium of internal revelation of God to you, the common language of the spirit of man, by which God communicates with your spirit.

INTERNAL REVELATION MADE INTELLIGENT BY INTERPRETATION

But if you want to make that medium of internal revelation of God intelligent to other folks, then it must be translated into the language that they know. That is the reason the apostle said, "*Let him that speaketh in an unknown tongue pray that he may interpret*" (1 Corinthians 14:13), so that the church may receive edifying. Paul also said, "*In the church I had rather speak five words with my understanding, that by my voice I might teach others also, than ten thousand words in an unknown tongue*" (1 Corinthians 14:19). Your revelation from God is given to you in tongues, but you give it forth in the language the people understand.

Beloved, settle it. It is one of the divine mediums and methods of communication between your spirit and God. And as long as you live, when you talk about tongues, speak with reverence, for it is God. When you talk about healing, speak with reverence, for it is God. When you talk about prophecy, remember, it is God.

AN ILLUSTRATION

A German woman came to the healing rooms one day, and a brother prayed for her. She had been a schoolteacher, but she had had to give up her profession because of her eyesight. She came back some weeks later after having been alone for three weeks. She had never been in a religious service in her life where they speak in tongues and had no knowledge of the Scriptures on that line. She came back to me with a volume of written material that God had given her. When she had been prayed for to receive healing, the Spirit of God came upon her, and she was baptized in the Holy Ghost. And now, God had commenced to reveal Himself to her, teach her of His Word and of His will, until she filled a volume with written material of her conversations with God. She communed with God in tongues, her spirit speaking to God; but when she came to me, I received it in English.

The man who sits alongside of you cannot understand that. He never talked to God. He does not understand anything about getting up in the middle of the night to write down what God has said to him. Well, he needs something else to convince him that there is a God. *"Tongues are for a sign, not to them that believe, but to them that believe not"* (1 Corinthians 14:22). But prophecy, the speaking the message of

God, is for all. Therefore, Paul does not want them to crush a man who is speaking in tongues, but to keep their hands off and stand back. Leave him alone with God. Let him travel way out in God's love and power and come back with messages in his soul, but he must not monopolize the time of hundreds of people in the church with a private communication of God to his soul. But when he has completed his interview with God, he then gives forth his knowledge as interpretation or prophecy.

There have been so many controversies over the various gifts of the Spirit, as they appeared one after another. Twenty-five or thirty years ago, when we began in the ministry of healing, we had to fight to keep from being submerged by the opposition from our brethren in Jesus Christ who thought you were insane because you suggested that the Lord Jesus Christ could still heal. In the state of Michigan, I had to go into the courts to keep some of my friends out of the insane asylum because they believed God could heal without taking pills or some other material stuff. (To popularize healing, some have compromised on the use of medicines, but the real Christian still trusts God alone.)[11]

It was because they did not understand the eternal and invisible nature of God. They had no idea

---

[11.] Note: The viewpoint and emphasis expressed in this statement are those of John G. Lake. The statement may have been inserted after this sermon had been preached and transcribed.

God could be ministered through a man's hands and soul, fill a sick man's body, take possession of him, and make him whole. The world has had to learn this. It is a science far in advance of so-called material or physical science.

Then, that marvelous wave of God came over the country from 1900 to 1906 when hundreds of thousands of people were baptized in the Holy Ghost and spoke in tongues. But listen! Old John Alexander Dowie, riding on the wave of that wonderful manifestation of healing power, wanted to build a church and stamp it with healing only, and his church practically did that and died. Other churches branded theirs with holiness only and died; others with an anointing of the Holy Ghost branded theirs "baptism," and they also died in power. Later on, we wanted to build a great structure and stamp it with *tongues*. After a while, the tongues got dry. Somehow the glory and the glow had gone out of them. They became rattly and did not sound right.

What was the matter? Nothing was wrong with the experience. God had not departed from the life but was hidden from our view. We were absorbed in the phenomena of God and not in God Himself. Now we must go on.

Now, beloved, I can see as my spirit discerns the future and reaches out to touch the heart of mankind and the desire of God that there is coming from heaven a new manifestation of the Holy Ghost in power. That new manifestation will be in sweetness, in love, in tenderness, in the power of the Spirit, beyond anything your heart or mine ever saw. The very lightning of God will flash through men's souls. The sons of God will meet the sons of darkness and prevail. Jesus Christ will destroy antichrist.

A Deluge of the Spirit

In 1908, I preached at Pretoria, South Africa, when God came over my life one night in such power, in such streams of liquid glory and power, that I was conscious of it flowing off my hands like streams of electricity. I would point my finger at a man, and that stream would strike him. When a man interrupted the meeting, I would point my finger at him and say, "Sit down!" He fell as if struck and lay there for three hours. When he became normal, they asked him what happened, and he said, "Something struck me that went straight through me. I thought I was shot."

At two o'clock in the morning, I ministered to sixty-five sick people who were present. The streams of God pouring through my hands were so powerful that the people would fall as though they were hit. I was troubled because they fell with such violence. And the Spirit said, "You do not need to put your hands on them. Keep your hands a distance away." And when I held my hands a foot from their heads, they would crumple and fall in a heap on the floor. They were healed almost every one.

That was the outward manifestation. That was what the people saw. But, beloved, something transpired in my heart that made my soul like the soul of Jesus Christ. Oh, there was such tenderness, a newborn tenderness of God that was so wonderful that my heart reached out and cried and wept over men in sin. I could gather them in my arms and love them, and Jesus Christ flowed out of me and delivered them. Drunkards were saved and healed as they stood transfixed, looking at me.

During that period, men would walk down the aisle, and when they came within ten feet of me, I have seen them fall prostrate, one on top of the other. A preacher who had sinned, as he looked at me, fell prostrate, was saved and baptized in the Holy Ghost under my own eyes, as I preached or prayed.

I continued in the ministry of healing until I saw hundreds of thousands healed. At last, I became tired. I went on ministering, healing people day after day, as though I were a machine. And all the time, my heart kept asking, "O God, let me know You better. I want You; my heart wants You, God." Seeing men saved and healed and baptized in the Holy Ghost did not satisfy my longing soul. It was crying for a greater consciousness of God; the "withinness" of me was yearning for Christ's own life and love. After a while, my soul reached the place where I said, "If I cannot get God into my soul to satisfy the hunger in me, all the rest of this is empty." I had lost interest in it, but I put my hands on the sick, and they continued to be healed by the power of God.

I will never forget Spokane, Washington. During the first six months I was there, God satisfied the cry of my heart, and God came in and my mind opened and my spirit understood afresh, and I was able to tell of God and talk out of my heart like I never had been able to before. God reached a new depth in my spirit and revealed new possibilities in God.

So, beloved, you pray through. Pray through for this church; pray through for this work. Oh, God will come! God will come with more tongues than you have ever heard. God will come with more power than your eyes have ever beheld. God will come with waves of heavenly love and sweetness, and your heart will be satisfied in Him. Bless God!

Will a man speak in tongues when he is baptized in the Holy Ghost? Yes, he will, and he will heal the sick when he is baptized, and he will glorify God out of his spirit with praises more delightful and heavenly than you ever heard. He will have a majestic bearing. He will look like the Lord Jesus Christ and will be like Him. Blessed be God.

HOLY SPIRIT UNSELFISHNESS

The greatest manifestation of the Holy Ghost-baptized life ever given to the world was not in the preaching of the apostles; it was not in the wonderful manifestation of God that took place at their hands; it was in the *unselfishness* manifested by the church. Think of it! Three thousand Holy Ghost-baptized Christians in Jerusalem from the day of Pentecost onward, who loved their neighbor's children as much as their own, who were so anxious for fear their brethren did not have enough to eat that they sold their estates and brought the money and laid it at the apostles' feet! They said, "Distribute it; carry the glow and the fire and the wonder of this divine salvation to the whole world." (See Acts 2:44–45.) That showed what God had wrought in their hearts. Oh, I wish we could arrive at that place, where this church was baptized in that degree of unselfishness.

That would be a greater manifestation than healing, greater than conversion, greater than baptism in the Holy Ghost, greater than tongues. It would be a manifestation of the love of 1 Corinthians 13 that so many preach about but do not possess. When a man sells his all for God and distributes it for the kingdom's good, it will speak louder of love than the evangelists who harp about love and oppose tongues and the other gifts of the Spirit.

That was the same Holy Ghost who came upon them and caused them to speak in tongues. No more grabbing for themselves, no more bantering for the biggest salary, no more juggling to put themselves and their friends in the most influential positions. All the old characteristics were gone. They were truly loved. Why, their hearts were like the heart of Jesus, and their souls were like the soul of God. They loved as God loved: they loved the world, and they loved sinners so much that they gave their all to save them.

Do you want Him? You can have Him. Oh, He will come and fill your soul. Then the Holy Ghost will take possession of your life. He will reveal the wonder of heaven and the glory of God, and the richness and purity of His holiness, and make you sweet and godlike forever.

Thou are not far away, O God. Our souls are enveloped in the eternal God. We feel Thee round about us. We feel Thy precious, loving arm and the beating of Thy heart and the pulsing of Thy heavenly soul, and we are asking Thee, O God, that the truth of the Eternal shall be breathed into us forever, until all our nature is submerged in God, buried in God, infilled with God, revealing God.

Chapter Thirty-two

The Baptism of the Holy Ghost

Sermon Series

Sermon 2 of 3

The baptism of the Holy Ghost is a most difficult subject to discuss with any degree of intelligence; although we may not care to admit it, the fact remains that the density of ignorance among the people and the ministry on this subject is appalling. To view this subject with any degree of intelligence, we must view it from the standpoint of progressive revelation. Like Christian baptism, the operation of the Holy Ghost must be seen (comprehended) in its various stages of revelation. Otherwise, we shall be unable to distinguish between the operations of the Spirit in the Old Testament dispensation and the baptism of the Holy Ghost in the New Testament.

As we approach even the threshold of this subject, it seems as if the Spirit of God comes close to us. A certain awe of God comes over the soul. And it is my most earnest wish that no levity, satire, or sarcasm be permitted to enter into this discussion. Such things would be grievous to the tender Spirit of God.

In the beginning of this revelation, after the deluge, it seems as if God was approaching man from a great distance, so far had sin removed man from his original union with God at the time of his creation. God seems to reveal Himself to man as rapidly as man, by progressive stages of development, is prepared to receive the revelation. Consequently, we see that the baptism was a further revelation of God's purpose in purifying the heart from sin than was the original ceremony of circumcision. So the baptism of the Holy Ghost is a greater, more perfect revelation of God than was the manifestation of the Spirit in the Patriarchal or Mosaic dispensations.

Three distinct dispensations of God are clearly seen, each with an ever-deepening manifestation of God to man. A preceding dispensation of God never destroys a foregoing, richer revelation of God. This is manifestly seen in looking at the Patriarchal, Mosaic, and Christian dispensations.

In the Patriarchal dispensation, we see God appearing to man at long intervals. Abraham furnishes the best example, for God appeared to him at long intervals of twenty and forty years apart. It was the same with the other patriarchs.

Under the Mosaic dispensation, there is a deeper and clearer manifestation of God. God was ever present in the pillar of cloud and the pillar of fire. He was present also in the tabernacle, where the Shekinah glory overshadowed the mercy seat. This is a continuous, abiding revelation of God. It was God *with* man, not *to* man, as was the Patriarchal dispensation. God was leading, guiding, directing, forgiving, sanctifying, and abiding *with* man.

But the revelation of God under the Christian dispensation is a much deeper and truer revelation of God than this. It is God *in* man. It is the actual incoming of the Spirit of God to live in man. This brings us to where we can see the purpose of God in revealing Himself to man by progressive stages of revelation.

Man, by progressive stages through repentance and faith, is purified—not only forgiven for his transgressions, but also cleansed from the nature of sin within that causes him to transgress. This cleansing from inbred sin, the nature of sin, the carnal mind, the old man, etc., is the actual taking out of our breasts the desire for sin, and all correspondence with sin in us is severed. The carnal life is laid as a sacrifice on the altar of Christ in glad surrender by us. This inner heart cleansing that John and the disciples of Christ demanded is the work of the Holy Spirit by the blood and is necessary if maturity in Christ is to be achieved. A holy God must have a holy dwelling place.

Oh, wondrous salvation, wondrous Christ, wondrous atonement! Man, born in sin and shaped in iniquity, forgiven, cleansed, purified outside and inside by the blood of Jesus, and made the habitation (dwelling place) of God. It was so that man, once created in the likeness of God, should again become the dwelling place of God. That is what the atoning blood of Christ provided.

> *Christ hath redeemed us from the curse of the law, being made a curse for us: for it is written, Cursed is every one that hangeth on a tree: that the blessing of Abraham might come on the Gentiles through Jesus Christ; that we might receive the promise of the Spirit through faith.*
> (Galatians 3:13–14)

This reveals to us God's purpose, by the blood of Jesus Christ, for us now to become the habitation of God, "*in whom ye also are builded together for an habitation of God through the Spirit*" (Ephesians 2:22). Again, in 1 Corinthians 6:19, we see Paul in astonishment saying, "*What? know ye not that your body is the temple of the Holy Ghost?*" Let us now see where we are, and then we will better understand how to go on.

The Holy Ghost is the Spirit of God. His purpose is to dwell in man after man's perfect cleansing from sin through the blood of Jesus Christ. The Holy Ghost's coming was definite—just as definite as was the advent of Jesus. When Jesus was born, His birth was proclaimed by an angel voice and chanted by a multitude of the heavenly host praising God. (See Luke 2:9, 13–14.)

Equally so was the Holy Spirit's advent attested by His bodily form as a dove (see Luke 3:22) and by the sound from heaven as of a rushing mighty wind, and by the cloven tongues of fire upon each of them in the upper room. (See Acts 2:2–3.) Heavenly dove, tempest roar, and tongues of fire crowning the hundred and twenty were as convincing as the guiding star and midnight shout of angel hosts. The coming of the Holy Ghost upon the hundred and twenty is found in the second chapter of Acts.

At the Last Supper, when Jesus addressed the disciples, He said to them:

> *Nevertheless I tell you the truth; it is expedient for you that I go away: for if I go not away, the Comforter will not come unto you; but if I depart, I will send him unto you. And when he is come, he will reprove the world of sin, and of righteousness, and of judgment.* (John 16:7–8)

As the disciples were together at Jerusalem after the resurrection, when the two who had walked with Him to Emmaus were conversing with the eleven disciples, Jesus Himself stood in their midst. He said unto them, *"Peace be unto you"* (Luke 24:36). They were afraid, believing they had seen a spirit. Jesus addressed them and said unto them:

> *And, behold, I send the promise of my Father upon you: but tarry ye in the city of Jerusalem,*

273

until ye be endued with power from on high.
(Luke 24:49)

Then, in the first chapter of Acts, we find that the one hundred and twenty tarried in prayer in the upper room for ten days. Thus, there are fifty-three days from the crucifixion of Jesus to the day of Pentecost.

There was a crucifixion day. It was necessary. And now, we, the children of God, must be crucified with Christ and freed from sin; our old man must be nailed to the cross. We die to sin—a real act, a genuine experience—it is done. So we are made partakers of Christ's death.

But there was a resurrection day. Jesus arose as a living Christ, not a dead one. He lives. He lives. And by our resurrection with Him into our new life, we leave the old sin life and the old man buried in baptism (see Romans 6), and we are made partakers of His new resurrection life. The life of power, the exercise of the power of God, is made possible to us by Jesus, having elevated us into His own resurrection life by actual spiritual experience.

Then was His ascension—just as necessary as the crucifixion or the resurrection. Jesus ascended to heaven and sits triumphant at the right hand of the Father. And according to His promise, He sent upon us the Holy Ghost. This experience is personal and dispensational. The Holy Ghost descends upon us, entering into us, for the baptism of the Holy Ghost is the Holy God, the Spirit of Jesus, taking possession of our personalities, living in us, moving us, controlling us. We become partakers of His glorified life, the life of Christ in glory. So it was with the hundred and twenty.

> *And suddenly there came a sound from heaven as of a rushing mighty wind, and it filled all the house where they were sitting. And there appeared unto them cloven tongues like as of fire, and it sat upon each of them. And they were all filled with the Holy Ghost, and began to speak with other tongues, as the Spirit gave them utterance.* (Acts 2:2–4)

It was the Spirit who spoke in other tongues. What Spirit? The Holy Ghost, who had come into them, who controlled them, who spoke through them. Listen! Speaking in tongues is the voice of God. Do you hear God's voice? They spoke as the Spirit gave them utterance.

Now we have advanced to where we can understand God's manifestations—not God witnessing *to* man, not God *with* man, but God *in* man. They spoke as the Spirit gave them utterance.

He is the Christ, the Son of God. His atonement is a real atonement. Man again becomes the dwelling place of God.

Let us now see one of the most miraculous chapters in all the Word of God, Acts 10. A man, Cornelius, is praying. He is a Gentile centurion. An angel appears to him. The angel speaks. The angel says to send to Joppa for Peter. Peter is a Jew, and he is supposed to go into the home of a Gentile. He has not learned that salvation is for the Gentiles. God has to teach him. How does God do it?

Peter goes up on the housetop to pray, and as he prays, he is in a trance. Think of it—a trance. He falls in a trance. Suppose I fell on the floor in a trance. Nine-tenths of this audience would be frightened to death. They would instantly declare that my opponent [Du Toit] had hypnotized me. Why? Because of the ignorance among men of how the Spirit of God operates. But listen. Listen! As Peter lies on the roof in a trance, he sees a vision—a sheet let down from heaven, caught by the four corners, full of all manner of beasts and creeping things. And a voice—what voice? The Lord's voice—said, *"Rise, Peter; kill, and eat"* (Acts 10:13).

But Peter said, *"Not so, Lord; for I have never eaten any thing that is common or unclean"* (verse 14).

But the voice said, *"What God hath cleansed, that call not thou common"* (verse 15). Peter obeyed. He went with the messengers. Now see the result. As Peter spoke the Word, the Holy Ghost fell on all of them who heard the Word. *"And they of the circumcision which believed were astonished, as many as came with Peter, because that on the Gentiles also was poured out the gift of the Holy Ghost"* (Acts 10:45).

How did they know? *"They heard them speak with tongues, and magnify God"* (verse 46). Then Peter answered, *"Can any man forbid water, that these should not be baptized, which have received the Holy Ghost as well as we?"* (verse 47). And so it ended in a glorious baptismal service in water of all who had been baptized in the Holy Ghost.

In Acts 22:12, Paul tells of Ananias coming to see him, but how did Ananias know Peter was there?

And there was a certain disciple at Damascus, named Ananias; and to him said the Lord in a vision,...Arise, and go into the street which is called Straight, and inquire in the house of Judas for one called Saul, of Tarsus: for, behold, he prayeth. (Acts 9:10–11)

Now let us see that as we would see it today. The Lord said, "Ananias, go down into Straight Street to the house of Judas and ask for a man named Saul of Tarsus, because he is praying." And then the Lord told Ananias what Saul had seen:

And hath seen in a vision a man named Ananias coming in, and putting his hand on him, that he might receive his sight.

(Acts 9:12)

Here, Ananias talked with the Lord. Do you know anything of such communion or talks with God? If not, get the baptism of the Holy Ghost like the early Christians, and their knowledge and experiences afterward can be yours, and you will see as we do the operation of the Lord upon both saint and sinner by the Holy Ghost. Men ask us, "Where do you get your insight into the Word?" We get it just where Paul and Peter got it: from God, by the Holy Ghost. (See Galatians 1:11–12.)

Beloved, read God's Word on your knees. Ask God, by His Spirit, to open it to your understanding. Read the Word with an open heart. It is a lamp unto our feet and a light unto our path. (See Psalm 119:105.)

Ananias went as the Lord directed him and found Paul. And Paul was healed of his blindness and was baptized in the Holy Ghost and was also baptized in water and spoke in tongues *"more than ye all"* (1 Corinthians 14:18).

Now, let's look again at Acts 22. Ananias was speaking to Paul, and he said,

The God of our fathers hath chosen thee, that thou shouldest know his will, and see that Just One, and shouldest hear the voice of his mouth. For thou shalt be his witness unto all men of

what thou hast seen and heard. And now, why tarriest thou? arise, and be baptized, and wash away thy sins, calling on the name of the Lord. (Acts 22:14–16)

You see, as with Peter at Cornelius' house, all this work of the Spirit ended in salvation and baptism.

God, through Ananias, promised Paul that he should know *"his will, and see that Just One, and shouldest hear the voice of his mouth"* (Acts 22:14). When did that come to pass? Three years later, when Paul returned to Jerusalem: *"Then after three years I went up to Jerusalem"* (Galatians 1:18).

And it came to pass, that, when I was come again to Jerusalem, even while I prayed in the temple, I was in a trance. (Acts 22:17)

Think of it: the intellectual, wonderful Paul, the master theologian of the ages, the orator of orators, the logician of logicians, was in a trance. Bless God for that trance. It was the fulfillment of what Ananias had said to him three years before.

And saw him [Jesus] *saying unto me, Make haste, and get thee quickly out of Jerusalem: for they will not receive thy testimony concerning me.* (Acts 22:18)

Now, what is a trance? A trance is the Spirit taking predominance over the mind and body; and, for the time being, the control of the individual is by the Spirit. But, our ignorance of the operations of God is such that even ministers of religion have been known to say it is the devil.

Let us see where Paul got his commission to preach and instructions about what he was to preach and what his condition and attitude were when Jesus gave him his commission. (See Acts 26:16–18.) He was lying on the road on his way to Damascus. Now, if we were to see someone lying on the road talking to an invisible somebody, no doubt we would send for an ambulance or for the police in our ignorance. But this is where the glorified Christ spoke to Paul and gave him definite instructions about what he should preach, and the purpose of his preaching was to be the salvation, not the entertainment of others.

> *But rise, and stand upon thy feet: for I* [Jesus]
> *have appeared unto thee for this purpose, to*
> *make thee a minister and a witness both of*
> *these things which thou hast seen, and of those*
> *things in the which I will appear unto thee.*
>
> (Acts 26:16)

Jesus promised to appear to Paul again, and that was fulfilled while he lay in a trance in the temple three years later.

Now the object of his preaching was:

> *To open their eyes, and to turn them from dark-*
> *ness to light, and from the power of Satan unto*

God, that they may receive forgiveness of sins, and inheritance among them which are sanctified [present experience] *by faith that is in me* [Jesus]. (Acts 26:18)

From this, we see and are able to understand the operations of God by His Spirit. And now, is the Holy Ghost in the church today? Truly, He is, but you say, "We do not see Him work in this way." Why is it? Because you say all these things were for the apostolic days. You cannot take the Word of God and find one place where the gifts of the Holy Ghost were withdrawn.

The nine gifts of the Holy Ghost are found in the twelfth chapter of 1 Corinthians:

For to one is given by the Spirit the word of wisdom; to another the word of knowledge by the same Spirit; to another faith by the same Spirit; to another the gifts of healing by the same Spirit; to another the working of miracles; to another prophecy; to another discerning of spirits; to another divers kinds of tongues; to another the interpretation of tongues: but all these worketh that one and the selfsame Spirit, dividing to every man severally as he will. (1 Corinthians 12:8–11)

Oh, praise God for the discovery of the gifts of the Holy Ghost and especially for the gift of healing. May we all learn to know Christ, not only as our Savior, but as our Sanctifier and Healer, too.

Now I will go over these gifts on my fingers: first, wisdom; second, knowledge; third, faith; fourth, healing; fifth, miracles; sixth, prophecy; seventh, discerning of spirits; eighth, divers kinds of tongues; and ninth, the interpretations of tongues. We have seen that the Holy Ghost came into the church at Pentecost, and the gifts are in the Holy Ghost. Consequently, if the Holy Ghost came in the church, the gifts are here, too. Because of the lack of faith, we do not see them exercised in the ordinary church. We stand for the obtaining of the gifts of the Holy Ghost through our personal baptism in the Holy Ghost, and the enduement of the Holy Ghost power as promised by Jesus, yes, commanded by Him. *"Ye shall receive power, after that the Holy Ghost is come upon you"* (Acts 1:8).

People ask, "What is the gift of tongues?" Speaking in tongues is the voice (or operation) of the Spirit of God within. When the Holy Ghost came in, He spoke. Again, in Acts 10:44–48, when the Holy Ghost fell on them, Peter demanded the right to baptize them in water, saying, *"Can any man forbid water, that these should not be baptized, which have received the Holy Ghost?"* (verse 45); because *"they heard them speak with tongues, and magnify God"* (verse 46).

Tongues are the evidence of the baptism of the Holy Ghost—which, in turn, gives evidence of the person's salvation—by which Peter claimed the right to baptize them in water. Again, in Acts 19, Paul met twelve men at Ephesus whom John had baptized unto repentance, but now Paul baptized them again by Christian baptism. In verse 5, we read that when they heard Paul's message, they were baptized (water baptism) in the name of the Lord Jesus. And when Paul had laid his hands on them, the Holy Ghost came on them, and they spoke with tongues and prophesied. *"Tongues are for a sign, not to them that believe, but to them that believe not"* (1 Corinthians 14:22).

Chapter Thirty-three

The Baptism of the Holy Ghost and Some of the Things It Has Produced in My Life

Sermon Series

Sermon 3 of 3

The baptism of the Holy Ghost was of such importance in the mind of the Lord Jesus Christ that
He commanded His disciples to tarry in Jerusalem,
"until ye be endued with power from on high" (Luke
24:49). And they steadfastly carried out what the
Lord had commanded, waiting on God in a continuous prayer meeting in the upper room for ten days
until the promise of the Father was fulfilled (see Luke
24:49) and that baptism had fallen of which John the
Baptist spoke, saying,

> *I indeed baptize you with water unto repen-*
> *tance: but he that cometh after me is mightier*
> *than I, whose shoes I am not worthy to bear: he*
> *shall baptize you with the Holy Ghost, and with*
> *fire.* (Matthew 3:11)

In order to obtain from heaven the Spirit of Jesus (the Holy Ghost), it is first necessary that the individual shall know that his sins are blotted out, that the blood of Jesus Christ has sanctified his heart and cleansed him from the sinful or Adamic nature—the inherent nature of sin. (See Ephesians 2:1–3.)

Personally, I knew that my sins had been blotted out, but it was only two months prior to my baptism in the Holy Ghost that I learned by the Word of God and experienced in my life the sanctifying power of God subduing the soul and cleansing the nature from sin. This inward life-cleansing was to me the crowning work of God in my life at that point, and I shall never cease to praise God that He revealed to me, by the Holy Ghost, the depth of the power of the blood of Jesus.

Many inquire, "What is the reason that, when your heart is sanctified and the conscious knowledge of your cleansing has taken place, you are not instantly baptized with the Holy Ghost?" From my own experience and the experiences of others, it is readily seen that, notwithstanding that the heart is cleansed from sin, it is still necessary in many instances for the dear Lord to further spiritualize the personality until the individual has become sufficiently receptive to receive within his person the Holy Ghost. The forces of our personalities must be subdued unto God. This we commonly speak of as spiritualizing.

In many instances, even though the heart is really pure, yet the individual has not at once received the baptism of the Holy Ghost and sometimes has given up in despair and turned back to his first works, believing that there must still be sin in his heart, thus discrediting what God has already done within him through the blood of Jesus. No, it is not always that the heart is still impure. It is not because you are not thoroughly sanctified. It is only God waiting and working to bring you to the place and to spiritualize your personality sufficiently that you may receive the Holy Ghost into your being.

The baptism of the Holy Ghost is not an influence, nor yet a good feeling, nor sweet sensations, though it may include all of these. The baptism of the Holy Ghost is the incoming into your personality of the Holy Ghost, which is the Spirit of Jesus, taking real possession of your spirit (or inner man), of your soul (the mind and animal life), and of your flesh. He possesses the being. The flesh is caused to quake sometimes because of the presence of the Spirit of God in the flesh. Daniel and those around him quaked with great quaking when the Spirit of the Lord came upon him. (See Daniel 10:5–13.)

Beloved, do you realize that it is the Spirit of Jesus that is seeking admittance into your heart and life? Do you realize that it is the Spirit of Jesus within the spirit, soul, and body of the baptized believer who moves him in ways sometimes strange, but who accomplishes the wondrous work of God within the life that every baptized believer praises God has taken place in him?

While I was yet a justified man, even without an experience of sanctification, the Lord committed to me in a measure the ministry of healing inasmuch that many were healed, and real miracles of healing took place in some instances. Yet I did not know God as my Sanctifier. Ten years later, after sanctification had become a fact in my life, a great and wonderful yearning to be baptized in the Holy Ghost and fire came into my heart. After seeking God persistently almost night and day for two months, the Lord baptized me in the Holy Ghost, causing me to speak in tongues and magnify God.

I had looked for and prayed for and coveted the real power of God for the ministry of healing, and had believed God that, when I was baptized in the Holy Ghost, that His presence in me, through the Spirit, would do for the sick the things my heart desired and which they needed. Instantly upon being baptized in the Spirit, I expected to see the sick healed in a greater degree and in larger numbers than I had before known, and I seemed to be disappointed for a time.

How little we know of our own relationship to God! How little I knew of my own relationship to Him. Day by day, for six months following my baptism in the Holy Ghost, the Lord revealed to me many things in my life where repentance, confession, and restitution were necessary, and yet I had repented unto God long ago. Of the deep cleansing, the deep revelations of one's own heart by the Holy Ghost, it was truly as John the Baptist said,

> *Whose fan is in his hand, and he will thoroughly purge his floor, and gather his wheat into the garner; but he will burn up the chaff with unquenchable fire.* (Matthew 3:12)

First, then, I will say the baptism in the Holy Ghost meant to me a heart searching as I have never before known, with no rest, until the blood was consciously applied in every instance and my life set free from the particular thing that God had revealed. As I say, this process continued for six months after my baptism in the Holy Spirit.

Second, a love for mankind such as I had never comprehended took possession of my life. Yes, a soul-yearning to see men saved so deep, at times heart-rending, until, in anguish of soul, I was compelled to abandon my business and turn all my attention to bringing men to the feet of Jesus. While this process was going on in my heart, during a period of months, sometimes persons would come to my office to transact business, and even instances where there were great

profits to be had for a few minutes of persistent application to business, the Spirit of love in me so yearned
over souls that I could not even see the profits to be
had. Under its sway, money lost its value to me, and in
many instances I found myself utterly unable to talk
business to the individual until first I had poured out
the love-passion of my soul and endeavored to show
him Jesus as his then present Savior. In not just a few
instances, these business engagements ended in the
individual yielding himself to God.

That love-passion for men's souls has sometimes
been overshadowed by the weight of care since then,
but only for a moment. Again, when occasion demanded it, that mighty flame of love, absorbing one's whole
being in life, would flame forth until, on many occasions, under the anointing of the Holy Ghost, sinners
would fall in my arms and yield their hearts to God.

Others have sought for evidences of this Pentecostal
experience being the real baptism of the Holy Ghost.
Some have criticized and said, "Is it not a delusion?"
In all the scale of evidences presented to my soul and
taken from my experience, this experience of the divine love, the burning love and holy compassion of
Jesus Christ filling one's bosom until no sacrifice is
too great to win a soul for Christ, demonstrates to
me more than any other one thing that this is indeed
none other than the Spirit of Jesus. Such love is not

human! Such love is only divine! Such love is only Jesus Himself, who gave His life for others.

Again, I experienced the development of power. After the mighty love came the renewed, energized power for healing of the sick. Oh, what blessed things God has given on this line! What glorious resurrections of the practically dead! Such restorations of the lame and the infirm[12] and the blind! Such shouts of joy! Such abundance of peace! Verily, *"Himself took our infirmities, and bare our sicknesses"* (Matthew 8:17).

Then, the power to preach the Word of God in demonstration of the Spirit came as never before. Oh, the burning, fiery messages! Oh, the tender, tender, loving messages! Oh, the deep revelations of wondrous truth by the Holy Ghost! Preaching once, twice, sometimes three times a day, practically continuously during these four years and four months. Oh, the thousands God has permitted us to lead to the feet of Jesus and the tens of thousands to whom He has permitted us to preach the Word!

Next, the strong, forceful exercise of dominion over devils to cast them out came. Since that time, many insane and demon possessed have been set free, as spirits of insanity and all sorts of unclean demons have been cast out in the mighty name of Jesus through the power of the precious blood. Saints have

---

[12] *infirm*: feeble, weak. *Merriam-Webster's 11ᵗʰ Collegiate Dictionary* CD-ROM, © 2003.

been led into deeper life in God. Many, many have been baptized in the Holy Ghost and fire. Truly, the baptism in the Holy Ghost is to be desired with the whole heart.

Brother, sister, when we stand before the bar of God and are asked why we have not fulfilled in our life all the mind of Christ and all His desire in the salvation of the world, what will be our excuses if they are weighed against the salvation of imperishable souls? How terrible it will be for us to say we neglected, we put off, we failed to seek for the enduement that comes from on high—the baptism of the Holy Ghost.

Again, are we close with God? May we say that it was only after the Lord had baptized us in the Holy Ghost that we really learned how to pray? When He prayed through us, when the soul-cries, born of the Holy Ghost, rolled out of your being and up to the throne of God, the answer came back—His prayers, His heart-yearning, His cry. May God put it in every heart that we may indeed see the answer to our Lord's prayer: *"Thy kingdom come. Thy will be done in earth, as it is in heaven"* (Matthew 6:10).

But someone will ask, "How about tongues? We understood that you taught that tongues were the evidence of the baptism in the Holy Ghost." So they are. Tongues are a sign to them that believe not. (See

1 Corinthians 14:22.) While I personally praise God for the wonderful and blessed truths of His Word by the Spirit—revelations in doctrine, in prophecy, in poems by the Holy Ghost in tongues with interpretation—that He has given me, yet above all the external evidences, that which God accomplishes in your own life, demonstrating to your own consciousness the operations of God, no doubt is the great evidence to the believer himself. That which is known in consciousness cannot be denied. We stand firmly on scriptural grounds that every individual who is baptized in the Holy Ghost will and does speak in tongues.

Baptism means a degree of the Spirit upon the life sufficient to give the Spirit of God such absolute control of the person that He will be able to speak through him in tongues. Any lesser degree cannot be called the baptism or submersion and, we feel, could properly be spoken of as an anointing. The life may be covered with deep anointings of the Holy Ghost, yet not in sufficient degree to be properly called the baptism.

About the Author

John G. Lake

No words of mine can convey to another soul the cry that was in my heart and the flame of hatred for death and sickness that the Spirit of God had stirred within me. The very wrath of God seemed to possess my soul!

These words summarized the passion that propelled the lifelong ministry of John G. Lake. He spoke these words in reference to the intensity of emotion he felt as his thirty-four-year-old sister lay dying. He had already witnessed eight of his fifteen siblings die from illness; yet, he had also witnessed the miraculous healing of his own childhood rheumatoid arthritis, as well as a sister's breast cancer and a brother's blood disease, under the ministry of John Alexander Dowie. It was already too late to take this sister, who now lay at death's door, to Dowie's Healing Home in Chicago, so he telegraphed Dowie with a desperate plea for prayer. Dowie telegraphed back: "Hold on to God. I am praying. She will live." That simple declaration caused Lake to wage a furious spiritual attack on the power of death—and within the hour, his sister was completely healed.

It was battles such as this that brought John G. Lake face-to-face with his convictions. Was he going to stand by as the enemy took yet another loved one from him, or was he going to choose to stand in the enemy's way? Such an opportunity again presented itself on April 28, 1898, when his wife of five years lay dying. Jennie was battling for breath in her final hours when Lake finally put his foot down. He would not tolerate the enemy stealing away the mother of his children and his spiritual partner. He determined to believe God's Word as it was revealed to him for her healing. He contended for her life in prayer, and as a result, she rose up healed and praising the Lord in a loud voice. News of Jennie's miraculous healing spread, and from that time on, Lake was sought after for the power of his healing anointing.

John Graham Lake was born on March 18, 1870, in St. Mary's, Ontario, Canada. His parents moved the family of sixteen children to Sault Ste. Marie, Michigan, while he was still a young child. At the age of twenty-one, he became a Methodist minister; however, he chose to start a newspaper in Harvey, Illinois, instead of accepting a church ministry. From the newspaper business, Lake expanded his career pursuits by opening a real estate office in Sault Ste. Marie when he and his young, ailing bride returned there for her health.

In 1901, at the age of thirty-one, Lake moved to Zion, Illinois, to study divine healing under John Alexander Dowie. In 1904, Lake decided to relocate to Chicago, buying himself a seat on the Chicago Board of Trade. He was able to accumulate over $130,000 in the bank and real estate worth $90,000 within a year's time. This prompted the notice of top business executives who asked Lake to form a trust of the nation's three largest insurance companies for a guaranteed salary of $50,000 a year. He was now a top business consultant to top business executives, making money through hearty commissions as well. By turn-of-the-century standards, John Lake was making a fortune.

During his business life, Lake had made it a practice of speaking somewhere practically every night, after which he joined like-minded friends in seeking the baptism in the Holy Spirit. Finally, in 1906, while he and another minister were praying for an invalid woman, he experienced profound "currents of power" rushing through his entire being, and the woman was instantaneously healed.

Such was the power of his anointing that he wrote about it as being like the lightning of Jesus: "You talk about the voltage from heaven and the power of God! Why, there is lightning in the soul of Jesus! The lightning of Jesus heals men by its flash! Sin dissolves and disease flees when the power of God approaches!" Lake would also compare the anointing of God's Spirit to the power of electricity. Just as men had learned the laws of electricity, Lake had discovered the laws of the Spirit. And, as God's "lightning rod," he would rise within God's calling to electrify the powers of darkness and solidify the body of Christ.

For a while, Lake was able to juggle his great secular success and his growing desire for God. He had learned to walk in the Spirit as he described: "It became easy for me to detach myself from the course of life, so that while my hands and mind were engaged in the common affairs of every day, my spirit maintained its attitude of communion with God." But by 1907, he yielded to the call to full-time ministry, and he and Jennie disposed of their bank accounts and all real estate holdings by giving everything away to charity. From that point on, the Lakes relied on God alone for provision as they traveled the country ministering.

By January 1908, they began praying for the necessary finances to take their team to Africa. In April of that same year, the Lakes and their seven children left for Africa with only enough money to pay for passage on the ship. In faith, they believed God for the finances necessary to gain them admittance into the country and for provision once they arrived. The Lord provided exactly what they needed as they were lining up to pay the South African immigration fees in order to leave the ship. Before the family even left the dock once they had disembarked, a miraculous housing offer presented itself. They immediately settled into a furnished home in Johannesburg.

Days later, John was asked to fill in for a South African pastor who was taking a leave of absence. Over five hundred Zulus were in attendance his first Sunday in the pulpit, and as a result, revival broke out to such an extent that, within weeks, multitudes in the surrounding area were saved, healed, and baptized in the Holy Spirit. The success astounded Lake so much that he wrote: "From the very start, it was as though a spiritual cyclone had struck." In less than a year, he had started one hundred churches.

Ministry success came at a price, however. Before the year was out, on December 22, 1908, Lake came home to find Jennie had died. He was devastated. Early in 1909, he returned to the States to recuperate, raise support, and recruit new workers. By January 1910, he was headed back to Africa in the midst of a raging plague there. He was among the few who ministered to the sick and dying. He proved to local physicians that the germs would not live on his body due to the Holy Spirit alive in him. He actually verified this under a microscope, showing that the germs died upon contact with his body. Those who witnessed the experiment stood in amazement as Lake gave glory to God, explaining that: "It is the law of the Spirit of life in Christ Jesus. I believe that, just as long as I keep my soul in contact with the living God so that His Spirit is flowing into my soul and body, no germ will ever attach itself to me, for the Spirit of God will kill it."

In 1912, after five years of ministry in Africa, having produced 1,250 preachers, 625 congregations, and 100,000 converts, Lake returned to the United States. In 1913, he married Florence Switzer, with whom he had five children. They settled in Spokane, Washington, where they founded the Spokane Healing Home and Apostolic Church, which drew thousands from around the world for ministry and healing. In May 1920, the Lakes left Spokane for Portland, Oregon, where he started another similar apostolic church and healing ministry.

By 1924, Lake was known throughout America as a leading healing evangelist. He had established forty churches throughout the United States and Canada, in which there had been so many healings that his congregations nicknamed him "Dr." Lake.

In 1931, Lake returned to Spokane at the age of sixty-one. He was weak with fatigue and nearly blind. God ultimately restored his vision after Lake had a "talk" with the Lord about it. Sadly, after returning from a church picnic on Labor Day 1935, John G. Lake went home to be with the Lord. He was sixty-five years old.

About the Compiler

Roberts Liardon

Roberts Liardon, author, public speaker, spiritual leader, church historian, and humanitarian, was born in Tulsa, Oklahoma, the first male child born at Oral Roberts University. For this distinction, he was named in honor of the university founder. Thus, from the start of his life, Roberts was destined to be one of the most well-known Christian authors and speakers of the turn of the millennium. To date, he has sold over six million books worldwide in over fifty languages and is internationally renowned.

An author of over four dozen Christian and self-help books, Roberts began his career in ministry when he gave his first public address at the age of thirteen. At seventeen, he published his first book, *I Saw Heaven*, which catapulted him into the public eye. By the time he was eighteen years old, he was one of the leading public speakers in the world.

Roberts's notoriety increased outside Christendom, as well. Twice he was voted Outstanding Young Man in America, and his career has taken him to over one hundred nations around the world, having been hosted by presidents, kings, political and religious leaders, and other world dignitaries.

In 1990, at the age of twenty-five, Roberts established his worldwide headquarters in Southern California, which became a base for his humanitarian work. He has trained, financed, and sent forth more than 250 men and women to various nations. These humanitarian missionary teams have taken food, clothing, and medical supplies, along with the message of Jesus, to needy friends and neighbors worldwide.

As a church historian, Roberts fervently researches our Christian heritage. At age twelve, he received instruction from God to study past heroes of faith and gain insight into their successes and their failures. The pursuit of Christian history became his passion, and, even as a young man, Roberts spent much of his free time with older Christians who knew the likes of William Branham, Kathryn Kuhlman, and Aimee Semple McPherson—great men and women of faith whose stories are told in the first *God's Generals* book and videos. Roberts possesses a wealth of knowledge regarding the great leaders of three Christian movements—Pentecostal, divine healing, and charismatic—and has established ongoing research through the Reformers and Revivalists Historical Museum in California.

Overall, historian, pastor, teacher, humanitarian, and philanthropist Roberts Liardon has dedicated his entire life and finances to the work of God's kingdom and the welfare of his fellow man, keeping a watchful eye on those less fortunate and doing all he can to ease their pain and help their dreams come to pass.

Since 2000, Roberts has worked to fulfill a demanding speaking schedule, along with writing new books and mentoring a new generation of world leaders to effect change for the church and society. He continues to manage and expand his international headquarters in Sarasota, Florida, and has an extension office in London, England.

Contact Information

USA:
Roberts Liardon Ministries
P.O. Box 2989
Sarasota, FL 34230

United Kingdom/Europe:
Roberts Liardon Ministries
22 Notting Hill Gate
Suite 125
London, UK W11 3JE

On the Web:
www.robertsliardon.org • www.godsgenerals.org